AST

Charles Harvey has been a full-time astrologer and teacher for over 30 years. He is co-ordinator with Liz Greene of The Centre of Psychological Astrology.

Suzi Harvey is a consultant astrologer, counsellor and editor of the prestigious Astrological Journal.

They are the authors of the much acclaimed *Sun Sign, Moon Sign*.

THORSONS
PRINCIPLES
OF

ASTROLOGY

CHARLES AND SUZI HARVEY

Thorsons
An Imprint of HarperCollins*Publishers*

Thorsons
An Imprint of HarperCollins*Publishers*
77–85 Fulham Palace Road
Hammersmith, London W6 8JB

Published by Thorsons 1999

10 9 8 7 6 5 4 3 2 1

A catalogue record for this book is available
from the British Library

ISBN 0 7225 3364 0

Printed and bound in Great Britain by
Caledonian International Book Manufacturing Ltd, Glasgow

TO ALL WHO WOULD HEAR
THE MUSIC OF THE SPHERES.

CONTENTS

ACKNOWLEDGEMENTS

O ur grateful thanks to the Urania Trust and their web site, for supplying and checking the information in the Resources section of this book. We are indebted to our many students over the years at both the Faculty of Astrological Studies' summer schools at Jesus College, Oxford, and at the Centre for Psychological Astrology for their refreshing insights and ever different approaches to this universal subject. Specific thanks are due to Dr.Will Keepin for permission to quote from his Interview in *The Mountain Astrologer*, Feb/March 1997 and to Dr Richard Tarnas, Professor of Philosophy and Psychology at the California Institute of Integral Studies for permission to quote from his forthcoming book *Cosmos and Psyche: Intimations of a New World View*, Random House, New York, 1999. Grateful acknowledgement also to the estate of Jeff Mayo for permission to reproduce an astronomical diagram from his *Astrologer's Astronomical Handbook*. Special thanks are due to our editor Michele Turney for all her work in helping to tighten up and clarify the text of this book and to Michelle Pilley for her original interest and encouragement and for her patience whilst the book was gestating.

1

THE ASTROLOGER'S UNIVERSE

Whatever is born or done this moment of time has the qualities of
this moment of time.

C.G. JUNG

Time is the flowing Image of the Eternal ... and the planets are
the instruments of Time.

PLATO, THE *TIMAEUS*

THE STUDY OF TIME

B ehind the light-hearted horoscopes of the popular press
lies a hidden wisdom that can transform our understanding of ourselves and the nature of reality. For *real*
astrology, from which this popular entertainment derives, is a
language, science, art and craft that deals with the ever-changing
qualities of time. Astrology studies the paradox that in each
moment of space-time there is a point of access to the Eternal. It
shows that each moment, such as of our own birth, is a seed
containing a specific blueprint for the unfoldment of the infinite potential of one facet of the Great Jewel of Eternity.

Normally we take time for granted; we think of it as something neutral and simply a measure of duration. But in fact,

according to the astrological and Platonic tradition, time is the great formative dimension of life. It is the dimension of time which, by means of the planetary cycles, dictates and unfolds into manifestation the changing patterns of Divine Ideas that shape our individual mind-set. It is the cycles of time, such as the daily shift from dark to light, and of the seasons, which govern the ebb and flow of daily life and at the same time the rise and fall of civilizations and the evolution of consciousness.

If this is your first astrology book, make a note of the time, date and place you obtained it. As you progress in your study of time, you will be amused and instructed by looking back at a map of this moment of space-time to see how it relates to your own birth chart, the unfoldment of your own consciousness of your infinite yet very specific potential.

A NOBLE SECRET

It is deeply unfortunate that for much of the general public the word astrology instantly means the Lottery's Mystic Meg and breathless mediums peering into crystal balls. As the great French surrealist poet, critic and philosopher André Breton (1896–1966) lamented:

> I see astrology as a very great lady, most beautiful, and coming from such a great distance that she cannot fail to hold me under her spell. In the purely physical world, I see nothing that has assets to emulate hers. She seems to me, besides, to hold one of the noblest secrets of the world. What a shame then, that nowadays – at least for the common masses – a prostitute reigns in her place.

Since Breton wrote that, the media's trivialization of the 'very great lady' has become even more widespread. In consequence, no one who has not studied a book on real astrology could possibly understand why some of the very greatest minds and creative individuals down the centuries have preoccupied themselves with its study. From Pythagoras, Plato, Plotinus and Proclus to St Thomas Aquinas, Kepler, Galileo, Goethe, Ralph Waldo Emerson, W.B. Yeats and Jung and many, many more, the Royal Art and Science has proved to be a source of deep fascination, inspiration and guidance. And, despite the contemptuous guffaws of scientific orthodoxy, it still continues to enthral the minds of some of our finest contemporary thinkers, and to be used, behind the scenes, by some of the world's leading figures. So what is astrology's noble secret?

Astrology's noble secret is rooted in the fact that she preserves an ancient understanding of the temporal cosmos as:

- the flowing image of the Eternal God Thought;

- a living, intelligent, purposeful entity in which part and whole dance together in resonance to the music of the spheres;

- a hierarchy of levels of order in which the higher levels order the lower and in which the apparent random activity here on Earth below can be seen to be orderly behaviour when viewed from the heavens above.

We explore the key principles of this understanding of the cosmos in the next chapter. But first we need to look briefly at some of the key steps in the history of the evolving consciousness of the relationship between above and below, between time and eternity.

A BRIEF HISTORY

Prior to Newton, most thinkers in Western universities, and in most Eastern cultures, believed that all life on Earth was regulated and controlled by the movements of the celestial bodies. This was not a superstitious belief but a position developed from reason and experience over 2,000 years, and one that is still maintained by thinking astrologers today. This does not contradict the laws of physics, which describe the material causes of things, because astrology is concerned with those metaphysical laws that describe the formal causes of things. Whilst some early astrologers certainly thought in terms of physical 'influences', the philosophers thought in terms of the cosmos as 'a living body of ideas'. How did this world view develop?

EARLY ORIGINS – ORDER OUT OF CHAOS

The early history of astrology can be only a matter of conjecture. What we do know is that the very earliest records in most cultures and civilizations reveal an essentially astrological world-view. Around 7,500 BCE in Europe, reindeer antlers were being used to note the phases of the moon, whilst the development of writing in Mesopotamia around 3,500 BCE was initially primarily concerned with recording celestial phenomena and their significance. Likewise, all major ancient buildings, such as the Ziggurats of Mesopotamia, the Egyptian and Mayan Pyramids, and Neolithic circles like Stonehenge, seem to have been constructed to align society below with the heavens above.

As early humankind came to consciousness, what became apparent amongst the seeming arbitrariness of life was the regularity of the cycles of day and night, of the waxing and waning of the moon and the movements of the planets across the star-studded sky. It was seen that these regular and predictable cycles of heaven could be related to natural phenomena such as the recurring seasons, the flooding of rivers, outbreaks of disease and years of feast and famine. Likewise the birth of distinct types of people and different kinds of destiny were observed to correspond with particular patterns of the planets.

Astrology appears to have emerged independently in different cultures around the world. Whilst some of these astrologies certainly cross-fertilized one another, each seems to have had the same basic insight about the intimate relationship between above and below. Likewise the essential significance of the planets and stars is very similar in different traditions. Mars is always associated with fire, anger and war, whilst Venus is seen to be an essentially beneficent creature of beauty.

The earliest written records of astrology are found in Mesopotamia where celestial events such as eclipses and the conjunction of planets were observed to be omens of coming events. The discovery of the cycle of the seasons and the fact that different times were good for different kinds of activities may well have encouraged pastoral settlements. It certainly enhanced the efficiency of agriculture in Egypt as the rising of certain stars just before the Sun could be used to time the flooding of the Nile.

ASTROLOGY IN THE BIBLE

The Bible, which is replete with astrology, preserves the deep understanding of the importance of time. Thus at the outset, Genesis 1:14–15, we find God on the fourth day saying:

> Let there be lights in the firmament of the heavens to divide the day from the night; and let them be for signs, and for seasons, and for days, and years...

Much later, in Ecclesiastes 3, we find the view summarized in the 16-line poem beginning:

To everything there is a season
And a time to every purpose under the heavens
A time to be born, and a time to die;
A time to plant, and a time to pluck up that which is planted;
A time to kill, and a time to heal;
A time to break down and a time to build up;
A time to weep, and a time to laugh;
A time to mourn, and a time to dance …

THE THREE WISE MEN

Astrology is central to the Judaeo-Christian tradition. The Three Wise Men of the Bible who 'followed the Star' were of course astrologers, a translation now used in *The New English Bible*. The particular 'star' the Magi were following was almost certainly the dramatic conjunction of the planets Jupiter and Saturn in Pisces, the sign of the fishes. This occurred three times in 7 BCE, which is now agreed to have been the most likely year of Christ's birth. Such a thrice-repeated conjunction was of especial significance to the ancient astrologers, and the symbology of the fish is ubiquitous in early Christianity. Christ, the 'fisher of men', was known as ICTHUS (Jesus Christ Son of God). To this day bishops wear a fish-tailed mitre. What is also clear from the Bible is that there have always been 'false prophets' who have used astrology for dubious purposes.

UNDERSTANDING THE COSMIC ORDER
– THE GREEKS

Early astrology may have emerged in part from observation, but certainly it seems reasonable to conjecture that the basic insight of the correspondence of above and below will have derived from the intuitive inner illumination of priests and shamans who saw this reality within themselves. The Greeks, starting with Pythagoras (*c.* 600–540 BCE), who emphasized the importance of number as the basis of the world, began to put in place a systematic model of an astrological universe. This was first fully articulated by Plato in the *Timaeus*. This ideal, transcendant model, interwoven with its rational, empirical, Aristotelian complement, was the basis of the prevailing world-view until the 17th century.

The history of the progress of this world-view would require another volume. A few of the important individuals and events are summarized below.

Some Highlights of Astrological History

Pythagoras (*c.* 580–*c.* 500 BCE) teaches that number is the creative basis of the cosmos and that each planet has its note, together producing the Music of the Spheres.

Empedocles (*c.* 490–430 BCE), Greek philosopher, proposes that all things, including human personality, are made up of the four elements Fire, Earth, Air and Water.

Hippocrates (*c.* 460–377 BCE), physician and astrologer, the 'Father of medicine', relates the four elements to the four humours as the basis of disease.

Plato (*c.* 427–347 BCE) elaborates the basis of astrology in the *Timaeus*; *c.* 387 BCE founds his philosophical Academy in Athens which lasts until 529 CE.

409 BCE – First known individual horoscope.

356 BCE – Alexander the Great's mother instructed by the astrologer Nectanebus as to when to give birth to the future Emperor: 22 July 356 BCE c. 11 p.m. in Mella, Macedonia.

Zeno (c. 342–c. 270 BCE), Syrian Stoic philosopher, teaches the cyclic nature of the universe and the importance of understanding the birth chart to free oneself from fate.

Berossus (*fl.* 280 BCE) opens a school of astrology on Kos around 280 BCE.

Hipparchus (c. 190–120 BCE), Greek astronomer/astrologer, discovers the precession of the equinox, develops the rulerships of the parts of the body by the zodiac.

Philo of Alexandria (20 BCE–50 CE) attributes seven planets to parts of head, soul and body and develops concept of seven-year rhythm in life.

Thessalos (*fl.* 50 CE), physician and astrologer, sets out rules for herb gathering.

Ptolemy (c. 100–180 CE), astrologer-astronomer, writes his *Tetrabiblos* (c. 150 CE) summarizing most of the astrological knowledge of his age.

Plotinus (c. 205–c. 270 CE) – his *Enneads*, edited by the astrologer Porphry (c. 232–c. 305 CE), set out the foundations of Neo-Platonism in which astrology can flourish.

Iamblichus (255–330 CE) incorporates the mystery teachings of the Egyptians, Assyrians, Babylonians and Chaldeans into Neo-Platonic thought.

Firmicus Maternus writes eight-volume astrology text *Mathesis libri* c. 335 CE.

Paulus Alexandrinus c. 370 CE writes an *Introduction to Astrology*.

Proclus (410–85 CE), philosopher and astrologer. His *Theology of Plato* elaborates on the role and significance of the planetary gods.

Simplicius (531–79 CE) writes *Commentary on the Enchiridion of Epictetus* and about the relationship of the soul to the body and astrology.

529 CE Closure of the Platonic Academy in Rome by Justinian after 1,000 years forces Neo-Platonists with their understanding of astrology into exile in Asia Minor.

625–c. 700 CE The rise of Islam and spread of Islamic Empire brings the Neo-Platonic and Jewish and Indian teachings back into the West.

770–73 CE **Caliph al-Mansur** has the Indian *Siddhanda* translated into Arabic, so beginnng Moslem astrological tradition.

Abu Ma'shar (787–886 CE) writes his *Introduction to Astrology*.

Al-Biruni (973–1048 CE), mystical astrologer.

Ibn Junus (died 1009 CE), produces the Hakemite Planetary Tables.

1010–1027 CE *Liber Planetis et Mundi Climatibus* – the first European astrological text.

Guido Bonati (1210–1300), court astrologer to Frederick II, develops mid-points.

Roger Bacon (1216–94) sees the heavens as the organizing cause of all things.

Thomas Aquinas (1225–74) sets out the place of astrology in the scheme of things.

Petrarch (1304–74) reawakens the world to the cultural riches of the Graeco-Roman culture.

1398, 19 September Chancellor of Sorbonne in Paris attacks astrology.

Marsilio Ficino (1433–99) in his *De vita coelitus comparanda* expounds on the value of astrology in daily life.

Regiomontanus, Johann Müller (1436–61), astrologer and 'Father of German astronomy', recovers and translates key Greek astronomical/astrological texts.

Pico della Mirandola (1463–94) denounces the abuses of astrology.

Nicolaus Copernicus (1473–1543), founder of heliocentric astronomy, an astrologer.

Paracelsus (1493–1541), doctor, philosopher and astrologer, teaches that medicine without astrology is pseudo-medicine.

Michel Nostradamus (1503–66), physician and astrologer to Catherine de Medici.

Tycho Brahe (1546–1601), astronomer, sought to reform astrology.

Francis Bacon (1561–1656), philosopher and Lord Chancellor of England, advocates the use of astrology in medicine and weather-forecasting.

Galileo (1564–1642), astronomer and practising astrologer.

Johannes Kepler (1571–1630), astronomer and astrologer; discovers laws of planetary motion; works to demonstrate and reform astrology.

Dr John Dee (1527–1608), scholar, astrologer, spy (original 007), chief adviser to Queen Elizabeth I – elects her coronation chart.

William Lilly (1602–81), the first astrologer to write in English, forecasts Great Fire of London.

Placidus de Titis (1603–68), scholar, physician and astrologer.

Elias Ashmole (1617–92), scholar and astrologer, founder of Ashmolean Museum, Oxford.

Sir Isaac Newton (1642–1727) ends his days studying alchemy, a subject steeped in astrological method.

From about 1700, astrology began to fade from the map of mainstream knowledge, eclipsed by the excitement of discoveries in the material sciences which became the focus of intellectual exploration. The serious study of astrology survived amongst individual students and practitioners rather than in academia, though there were individual intellectuals who publicly espoused it. This was especially the case in Germany where the great German poet, writer, scientist and polymath Goethe (1749–1832) studied astrology and opened his autobiography with details of his birth chart which he considered a good description of his basic nature. The philosopher August Wilhelm Schegel (1767–1854) taught that 'astronomy will have to become astrology again', and the last university professor of astrology in Europe, Johann Wilhelm Pfaff (1774–1835), called for its recognition as a legitimate science in his *The Rationale of Astrology*. Arthur Schopenhauer (1788–1860), the philosopher, moved from a hostile position in his early work to a more sympathetic view in his *On Age Difference*. In the USA Ralph Waldo Emerson (1803–82), the philosopher with Neo-Platonic leanings, was sympathetic to astrology, describing it as 'astronomy brought down to earth and applied to the affairs of man'.

When the study of astrology faded, it was still part of mainstream thought; but when it began to re-emerge as a subject for popular study in the late 19th century, it was as a result of the efforts of relatively few maverick individuals working from outside the boundaries of orthodox study. Throughout the 20th century it has gradually developed and progressed into its present highly sophisticated form as the result of the work of a series of dedicated individuals and organizations. Some of the highlights of this story are shown below.

The Renaissance of Astrology

Richard Garnett (**1835–1906**), Keeper of Printed Books at the British Museum, advocates the use of astrology.

1880 A.J. Pearce (**1840–1923**) edits *Urania* and other journals. His *The Textbook of Astrology* takes a pragmatic and experimental approach to its development.

Walter Gorn Old/Sepharial (1864–1929) writes many books on astrology.

1888 Paul Choisnard/Flambert (1867–1920) starts statistical research in astrology.

1890 Alan Leo/William Frederick Allen (1860–1917) and F.W.Lacey found the monthly *Modern Astrology* (1890–1943). Leo goes on to publish a series of books with strong theosophical slant covering most known areas of astrology.

1915 13 July, 7.15 p.m., Alan and Bessie Leo found The Astrological Lodge of the Theosophical Society, the 'mother' of British astrology.

1926 The first issue of the Lodge's *Astrology Quarterly* edited by Charles Carter (1887–1968), philosopher and experimentalist who wrote widely on astrology.

1928 The first *Cosmobiology Yearbook* published in Germany. Alfred Witte in Hamburg publishes his *Regel für Planetenbilder* (*Rules for Planetary Pictures*).

1930 31 August, *Sunday* Express publishes R.H. Naylor's article on Princess Margaret's birth – the start of astrology in the popular press: soon spreads world-wide.

1936 Dane Rudhyar's *The Astrology of Personality* starts psychological astrology.

1939 Karl Ernst Krafft – *Traite d'Astro-biologie*; American Federation of Astrologers founded (May).

1940 Reinhold Ebertin in Germany publishes the first edition of *Kombination der Gestirneinflusse* (*Combination of Stellar Influences*).

1948, 7 June, 7.58 p.m., The Faculty of Astrological Studies founded to provide a systematic education for astrologers – world-wide via correspondence courses.

1955 – Michel Gauquelin publishes *L'Influence des Astres* demonstrating statistically that planetary positions at birth are related to future eminence in different professions.

1958, 21 June, 8.22 p.m., The Astrological Association founded by John Addey (1920–82), Brigadier General R.C. Firebrace and Joan Rodgers; Rudolf Tomaschek (1895–1966), Professor of theoretical physics at Munich, Chair of Cosmobiological Academy Aalen, publishes *Observations on the Basic Problem of Astrology*.

1959 *The Astrological Journal* of the Astrological Association first published.

1970 In London The Urania Trust, Educational Charity, created by John Addey *et al.*

1973 The Mayo School of Astrology founded by Jeff Mayo.

1974 In the USA, Neil F. Michelsen founds Astro-Computing Services and Dr Gregg Howe founds Astro-Numeric Services for astrologers.

1976 John Addey's *Harmonics in Astrology*; Liz Greene's *Saturn*.

1977 In the USA, astrology software for home computer from Michael Erlewine (1941–) and Robert Hand (1943–); Geoff Dean's *Recent Advances in Natal Astrology*.

1981 Astrology ceases to be illegal in Britain with the Repeal of the Vagrancy Act.

1983 In Zürich, Bruno and Louise Huber found the Astro Psychological Institute, API (8 June); in London, Liz Greene and Howard Sasportas (1948–93) found The Centre for Psychological Astrology – CPA (12 June); and Geoffrey Cornelius and Maggie Hyde the Company of Astrologers (14 November).

1985 Jim Lewis develops Astro*Carto*Graphy; first International Astrological Research Conference in London under the auspices of Professor H.J. Eysenck (1916–97).

1988 The Urania Trust creates the Astrology Study Centre in London and publishes first issue of the international Yearbook *Astrology*.

1990 In the USA, *Project Hindsight* launched by Robert Hand and Robert Schwarz to recover the ancient origins of astrology by the translated early Greek, Latin and Arabic text.

1996 *The Tenacious Mars Effect* by Ertel and Irving confirms Gauquelin's findings.

1997 *Cosmos and Culture* – journal for study of astrology in world culture launched.

1998 CPA launches *Apollon* – journal for psychological astrology.

THE WORK OF THE GAUQUELINS

No history of 20th-century astrology would be complete without mention of the remarkable work of the French psychologist and statistician Dr Michel Gauquelin (1928–91) and his demographer wife Françoise (1929–). Between them they gathered many tens of thousands of birth certificates of famous individuals from all over Europe. Birth certificates on the continent include the time of birth. Using this information, the Gauquelins were able to demonstrate statistically that eminent professionals tended to be born when particular planets were:

- close to the eastern or western horizon or

- close to the upper meridian, their highest point in the sky or

- close to the lower meridian, the lowest point.

For example, future champion athletes, eminent military men and entrepreneurs tend to be born when Mars, god of the warrior, is so placed. By contrast, the Gauquelins found that future eminent scientists tend to be born when Saturn, bestower of the saturnine cautious, methodical, intellectual temperament, is prominent. Future actors and politicians tend to be born when self-important, jovial Jupiter is in these positions. Future politicians are also found to be born with an angular Moon, as are future writers and journalists.

Despite attempts by several committees of sceptics to disprove these results, often using dubious methods, the observations have replicated again and again with fresh samples of data. An impartial survey of all the evidence by Suitbert Ertel, Professor of Psychology at Göttingen University in Germany, has concluded in *The Tenacious Mars Effect* that it is time that sceptics embraced the reality of these results and accepted the challenge they present to the prevailing world-view. Hans Eysenck, (1916–97), Professor of Psychology at London University and a strict experimentalist, came to the same conclusion.

EMERGING FROM ISOLATION

Astrology during the 20th century has been gradually emerging from 200 years of isolation. It is still not accepted by most academics, and encyclopaedias still omit it from the map of 20th century knowledge, or include it with scornful asides. Faced with the upsurge of interest in astrology, sociologists try to explain it as a superstitious reaction to the nihilism of the

20th century. Meanwhile, astrologers have simply got on with their work and have developed the study in exciting and philosophically challenging new areas. During the century, there has been a growing number of intellectuals who have slipped through the ring fence of academic scorn and now experiment with astrology.

The great Irish poet, dramatist and philosopher W.B. Yeats (1865–1939) studied and used astrology daily throughout much of his adult life. C.G. Jung (1875–1961), the great Swiss psychologist, was a pioneer in this area and wrote to Sigmund Freud:

> My evenings are taken up very largely with astrology. I make horoscopic calculations in order to find a clue to the core of psychological truth.

Likewise, in Austria, Oscar Adler, the medical doctor and musician brother of the great psychologist Alfred Adler, was a pioneer of modern astrology, and wrote a four-volume work, *An Astrologer's Testament*. Also in Austria, the philosopher and painter Thomas Ring (1892–1983) wrote and lectured widely on astrology throughout his life. In Germany between the wars, the traveller and philosopher Count Herman Keyserling (1880–1946) embraced astrology and wrote an important introduction to the subject, whilst his son, Arnold Keyserling (1922–), Professor of Philosophy at the University of Vienna, and a humanistic psychologist, lectures and teaches regularly throughout Europe on astrology.

The late Dr James S. Williamsen (1941–88), a brilliant American mathematician resident at King's College Cambridge and the Oxford Computing Laboratory, summed up the nub of the matter. When asked why, as a penetrating student of artificial intelligence, he would stoop to study astrology, Williamsen replied:

If we truly want to create artificial intelligence then we must first understand the operations of the Mind which created our minds. From my studies it seems clear that astrology holds a key to understanding and mapping the workings of what from earliest times was known as the Divine Intelligence.

Such views on the implications of astrology are not only to be heard from questing scientists. Professor Dr L. Cunibert Mohlburg of the Vatican Institute of Archaeology forecast in his book *Candi's Letter to Tschu* that:

> If we look ahead it is already possible to say that Astrology seems destined to lead all other branches of knowledge out of the blind alley of unspiritual rationalism and materialism ... and effect the reconciliation that Science so ardently desires with Belief.

At the present time, a leading contemporary philosopher Dr Richard Tarnas, author of the much-acclaimed history of Western thought, *Passion of the Western Mind,* has said he believes that:

> Psychology textbooks of the future will look upon modern psychologists working without the aid of astrology as being like medieval astronomers working without the aid of a telescope.

OBJECTIONS TO ASTROLOGY

HOW COULD ASTROLOGY POSSIBLY WORK?

Whether you are a true believer, an open-minded enquirer, or a dyed-in-the-wool sceptic, astrology presents us with a problem. How could it possibly work? What possible connection can there be between the positions of the planets at the time of birth and our character and destiny, or between planetary

movements and the movements of the stock market, or major political changes?

Astrology certainly runs contrary to the approach of science over the past 300 years and more. Scientific success has bred arrogance, and media pundits with only the dimmest understanding of the history of ideas will speak derogatorily of astrology as a throwback to superstitious un-reason. In fact, of all subjects astrology still addresses the inherent reasonableness of life, as we shall see in the next chapter.

NEWSPAPER ASTROLOGY

Different newspapers give different forecasts from the same information. All too true. Most newspaper columns are light-hearted fun and pour out 'thoughts for the day' without too much reference to the cosmic climate. Even the best and most conscientious of newspaper astrologers is faced with trying to reduce a cosmic ocean of information into a single sip. This is soundbites gone mad, and horoscope columns imply that they contain far greater personal information than they could ever supply. That said, a particular period of time will, on average, be more stressful or advantageous for certain signs. Prevailing surges in energy or tense patterns will tend to be picked up by some types rather than others. But for any particular individual, the 'signals' are likely to be swamped out by more personal factors.

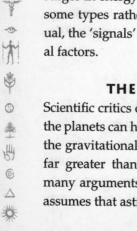

THE GRAVITY OF THE MIDWIFE

Scientific critics of astrology say that it is absurd to believe that the planets can have any effect on our character or destiny since the gravitational mass of the midwife in attendance at birth is far greater than any possible pull of the planets. This, like many arguments put forward by physicist critics of astrology, assumes that astrology is measuring material causes. In fact, as we shall see in the next chapter, it is clear that astrology measures the unfoldment of formal cause in the cosmos.

For example, the disillusionment with Communism and the impulse for political change which swept through Europe in 1989 as Jupiter opposed a tightening Saturn–Neptune conjunction had no physical gravity. The intellectual gravitas of these compelling ideas was more compelling than any number of secret police or border guards. The 'ideas of the time' swept all before them far more effectively than any hurricane or tidal wave. For astrologers, the cosmic configurations of that time 'birthed' a decisive new reality for the world.

PRECESSION OF THE EQUINOXES

The signs of the zodiac used by astrologers in the West are no longer the same as the constellations in the sky of the same name. This is perfectly true and all astrologers are aware of this fact. The Western tropical zodiac is measured from what astronomy calls The First Point of Aries, the point where the Sun crosses the Equator and follows the seasonal cycle. It measures unfolding life in relation to our Earth. The Fixed Zodiac of the Constellations measures out a larger more cosmic cycle of reference. Whilst this book focuses on the tropical zodiac, both frames of reference have their place in a larger astrology. An analogy might be that someone might be a Sun Leo in terms of their local political scene, a king: a big fish in a small pond. But when they graduate to national politics they get measured against another scale and may be a Sun Cancer, and a much less self-assured creature, a crab in a much vaster ocean.

THE STARS IN THE CONSTELLATIONS ARE OFTEN NOT PART OF THE SAME STAR SYSTEM

Astrology is not dependent on the constellations being all of a piece. No-one looking at the constellations and asked to make

pictures would see the animals and images that they are supposed to represent. It is clear that the ancients gave the names in order to summarize and symbolize their experience of planets moving through that part of the sky. The signs of the zodiac, whether tropical or fixed, tell a story of unfolding ideas which follows a particular sequence. In fact, there is also a branch of astrology which studies the significance of specific Fixed Stars. Again, the meaning of individual stars is based on observation and is in no way dependent upon it being part of a particular constellation.

HELIOCENTRIC RATHER THAN GEOCENTRIC

Since Copernicus it has been known that the Earth moves around the Sun and not vice versa. It is argued that astrology is Earth-centred and seems to assume that the planets move around the Earth. Astrologers are well aware of the distinction. In practice we live on the Earth and not the Sun, and in terms of the unfolding of planetary ideas for humankind it is therefore the Earth-centred view that is most relevant. There is, however, much to be learned from heliocentric astrology, which is a whole area of astrology in its own right.

Most objections to astrology come from individuals who can think only in terms of physical, material causes. Anyone who has worked in astrology for any length of time knows that astrology has to do with an algebra of meaning and consciousness rather than purely of matter.

Figure 1. The top diagram shows a top-down view of the solar system with the planets orbiting the Sun in the centre. This is the helio-centric view. The lower diagram shows how these same positions appear when seen from the earth as centre, the geocentric view.

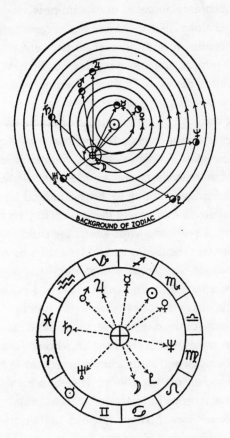

PHYSICAL THEORIES ABOUT ASTROLOGY

All that said, there are still some astrologers who can only feel comfortable with material causes. And there is a range of theories that have been elaborated to explain how astrology might work. The analogy of the Moon and ocean tides is often invoked. The human body is over 90 per cent water. Do the planets have minute tidal effects within our bodies?

Related to this theory is Dr Percy Seymour's eloquent resonance theory, which points out that resonance can give wave forms power out of all proportion to their inherent energy. Classic examples of this are the singer who can break a glass at a distance by singing the glass's 'note' so that it vibrates itself to pieces. Likewise an army marching over a bridge has to break step so as not to set the bridge vibrating to its own natural frequency and make it fall apart. In this model, the planets in their movements are setting up wave forms with which the child resonates and 'tunes in', thereby establishing certain types of behaviour.

Endocrinologist Dr Frank MacGillion has put forward endocrine secretions from the pineal gland as a possible mechanism, pointing out numerous studies which highlight the importance of the state of the day–night cycle at the time of birth and its effects on melatonin secretions. Dr Michel Gauquelin, the French psychologist and statistician, whose work is cited above, postulated a genetic predisposition, whereby a baby with a martial genetic make-up would be tuned to Mars orbit.

Such theories may perhaps explain certain very limited astrological phenomena. However elegant some of these theories are, though, they simply cannot explain how it is that a chart set for the moment of the formation of a company can provide detailed information about its likely company style, its development and the kind of people that it will attract to it.

In the next chapter we look at the central philosophical principles upon which astrology is traditionally based. Even if you are someone who would prefer a neat physical cause-and-effect model, you will find that if you engage with these ideas they will provide a framework within which to think about astrology.

THE ANCIENTS SAID IT ALL

The philosophy of the astrological world-view, which assumes an intimate, meaningful connection between the above and the below, has never been more eloquently expressed than by the writings attributed to the wise Egyptian Hermes Trismegistus. In this passage, the relationship of the Cosmic Principles to their Source is being explained to Hermes by the great Pymander: (from *The Divine Pymander of Hermes Trismegistus*, ed. The Shrine of Wisdom, 1970.)

Hermes Trismegistus: Many men have affirmed many and diverse things concerning the Cosmos and God, but I have not learned Truth; therefore, O Lord, make plain these things to me.

Pymander: Hear, then, my Son, how these things are of God and the Cosmos.

1. God; Eternity; the Cosmos; Time; Generation.

2. God maketh Eternity;

Eternity maketh the Cosmos;

The Cosmos maketh Time;

Time maketh Generation.

3. The Substance, or Essence, as it were, of God, is the Good, the Beautiful, Blessedness, and Wisdom;

of Eternity, is Identity and Sameness;

of the Cosmos, is Order;

of Time, is Change;

of Generation, is Life and Death.

4. The Operation, Energy, or Activity

of God, is in Nous and Soul;

of Eternity, is in Permanence and Immortality;

of the Cosmos, is in Integration and Re-integration;

of Time, is in Augmentation and Diminution;

of Generation, is in Qualities.

5. Therefore, Eternity is in God;

The Cosmos is in Eternity;

Time is in the Cosmos;

Generation is in Time.

6. Eternity abides with God;

The Cosmos is moved in Eternity;

Time is accomplished (i.e. has its limit) in the Cosmos;

Generation takes place in Time.

7. Therefore, the Source and Foundation of All is God, but the Essence of Substance is Eternity; and the Matter is the Cosmos.

8. The Power of God is Eternity; the Work of Eternity is the Cosmos, which is unmanifest and also ever being made manifest by Eternity.

9. Therefore the Cosmos shall never be destroyed, nor the things in it perish, for Eternity is indestructible, and the Cosmos is contained and encompassed by Eternity.

A CONTEMPORARY SYNTHESIS

At the end of the 20th century, the re-emergence of astrology challenges the Western mind once again to find a framework of thought that can resolve the tension that has existed since the Greeks – between Platonic idealism with its emphasis on consciousness and Aristotelian empiricism with its emphasis on matter. For, of all studies, astrology demands a philosophy and framework of thought that embraces both physics and metaphysics, the temporal and the eternal, the manifest and the unmanifest, the observed and the intuited, the material and the formal. The phenomena of astrology demand a model of the universe that is inclusive of quantity and qualities, matter and consciousness. Hermes Trismegistus's perspective, above, with its emphasis on the relation of the temporal to the eternal, offers such a resolution in principle. The problem, then, is to translate these insights into a form and language that is intelligible to contemporary thought.

One contemporary thinker who has embraced this challenge is Will Keepin, a nuclear physicist, whose mother and father were both nuclear physicists, who is also a practising astrologer. Keepin has been obliged by the reality of his astrological experience to engage with the resoltion of these worldviews. He finds a meeting place in the work of the late David Bohm, a student of Einstein, who was until recently Professor of Theoretical Physics at London University. In his book *Wholeness and the Implicate Order*, Bohm pictures the universe as having both an implicate, eternal, 'enfolded' order which is unfolded in the explicate order of space-time. Bohm sees each moment of space-time as both an explicit manifestation of a particular part of that implicate order and a point of access and linkage to that Wholeness. This evokes the holographic image of reality that we see reflected in the relationship between cells in a body and the body as a whole. In an interview in *The Mountain Astrologer*, February/March 1997, Keepin sums up the implications of Bohm's work and his own thinking as follows:

> Any natural science from physics to biology to astrology is basically an enterprise of pattern recognition, which utilizes a naturally existing order to discern replicable truths. So astrology is a science of the order in meaning, and the correlation between the subtle order and the Cartesian order in the physical motion of the planets.

For each point in space-time there is a unique astrological chart. I see the astrological chart as a kind of cosmic indexing of the unfolding cosmos. In this grand evolutionary process, each point in the emergent space-time is characterized by a unique astrological chart. It is almost as if the chart is an index for the creative process of cosmic evolution. And when one is born with a particular chart, one becomes an ambassador of sorts to the rest of the cosmos, representing a unique moment in the cosmic space-time to the rest of the cosmos as it continues to unfold.

Each one of us is expressing a particular aspect of the mystery and bringing it into fluid relationship with the rest of the unfolding mystery. Now in terms of astrology and the implicate order, I see the implicate order as a vast realm of meaning and purpose and all of the invisible and intangibles, including, at its deepest levels, the creative process of love itself.

The implicate order is essentially the whole of the unmanifest realm, and the laws that operate in that domain. Astrology is an attempt to map out some of the elementary workings in that domain, and it works by utilizing the non-Cartesian order and non-material laws that govern that domain.

When Keepin's perspective is put together with the insights of the great British astrologer, philosopher and mystic John Addey, who also draws on Bohm, as in *A New Science of Astrology*, a picture begins to emerge of astrology as a systematic algebra of life and consciousness which is entirely compatible with the new physics. But not only is astrology in accord with the new physics, it also has the power to reveal to physics and philosophy a profoundly potent dimension of reality which was familiar to the ancients but which has been all too long neglected and denied. This is the dimension of cosmic meaning, purpose and intention.

THE FIRST PRINCIPLES

Nothing exists nor happens in the visible sky that is not sensed, in some hidden moment, by the faculties of Earth and Nature.

JOHANNES KEPLER (1571–1630), FROM *DE STELLA NOVA*

The Cosmos is a living body of Ideas.

PLATONIC DICTUM

Astrology views the cosmos as an intelligent and harmonious whole. It sees it as being shaped and unfolded constantly by cyclical processes in which we, as conscious, reflective human beings, can participate. Whether we choose to reflect rationally on these cosmic processes or not, we participate in them intrinsically at every level of our being. This is the astrologer's world view – that we are each a universe in miniature. This chapter gives an overview of the first principles on which astrology is based – those principles which are at work in the world and within us.

UNITY

The great American astrologer Charles Jayne (1917–1989) described astrology as cosmo-ecology. This is very close to the truth, because at the heart of astrology is the concept that all things, from atoms to universes, are part of one another and of one over-arching *unity*. Part and whole are seen as identical in essence (but not in function), intimately connected and in continual resonance with each other. This cosmo-ecology is seen not only as applying to our Earth within the solar system, but equally to our solar system within our galaxy, around which our Sun carries us in about 230 million years. And again beyond the galaxy to the super-galaxies and super-super galaxies, 'wheels within wheels', extending outward to the ultimate oneness of the Infinite One.

This concept of unity is at the core of the words we use to describe the totality of things. The word cosmos comes from the Greek *kosmos*, meaning an orderly, beautiful harmony, as in the word cosmetics. Likewise the word universe comes from the Latin *uni-versum*, meaning 'to turn towards the One'. Hence, an ancient university was a place where one studied everything in relation to the One (i.e. the One Truth, the One Knowledge). In German we find the same concept in their word for cosmos, *das All*, the All, that which contains everything. Or again in English, we find it in that telling sequence of words *whole, hale, healthy* and *holy*, which are all from the same Anglo-Saxon root meaning to be whole, robust, at one with unity.

Plato, the father of Western philosophy, who set out the first philosophy of astrology in the *Timaeus*, sums up the primacy of this concept of Unity:

> Every diagram and system of number, and every combination of harmony, and the revolution of the stars, must be made manifest as the ONE THROUGH ALL to him who learns in the proper way. And it will be made manifest if, as we say, a man learns by keeping his gaze on Unity.

AS ABOVE, SO BELOW

As Above, So Below that the miracle of the Unity may be perpetuated.

HERMES TRISMEGISTUS, *THE EMERALD TABLETS*

Astrology studies the arrangement of planets in the solar system at a particular moment in order to determine the potential of an individual or other entity born at that moment.

In terms of current Western thought, this seems utterly irrational. Viewed holistically, it is entirely reasonable, for the universe is not only a unity in itself, it is a unity of unities. And, as the Platonists pointed out, 'all unities are identical in essence'. In this way, as the legendary Hermes indicates, 'the miracle of the Unity is perpetuated'.

The Cosmos itself, and each part of the cosmos including we human beings, is 'made in the image' of the ONE, the 'God Thought' which thinks creation into existence. In this way, the essential pattern of the ONE is both literally and metaphorically present in every part of Creation, from super-galaxy to solar system, to man, to a cell in the body, to an atom and to the last and least of things. Everything, in this sense, is a metaphor of the primary music of the One and the gods, the original Word.

These sound like very elevated ideas, and one might ask how we get from this sublime oneness down to the rest of the mundane world. That question belongs in another book, but suffice it to say that the ONE expresses itself at each level of creation in very different ways. We see this principle at work in genetics. Hence the possibility of cloning and the re-creation of an entity from a single cell of the original whole, an idea which was exploited to such dramatic effect in the film *Jurassic Park*. Every cell in an organism contains the instructions for making the whole organism. A blood cell and a skin cell and a hair cell contain identical genetic information, although their actual manifest functions are quite different. At the most basic level, they are each made 'in the image of the one', and yet each just gets on with its own job. The 'wholeness' of the body needs each cell to do just that.

Likewise, in the life cycle of, for example, a butterfly, it is impossible to see any obvious resemblance between a butterfly's egg, the caterpillar, the dried-up brown chrysalis, and the colourful new butterfly. Yet each phase leads on in an ordered, intelligent way to the next, and finally to the flowering of the whole organism; genetically each phase contains identical information.

By analogy, a galaxy and a solar system and a man or woman may look very different. But in real terms each is a different expression of the same basic 'God Thought'. This is what is meant by such cryptic statements as 'man is made in the image of God', 'man is a solar system in miniature', 'microcosm and macrocosm are identical in essence', and what Origen (AD 185–254) meant when he said 'Thou art a second world in miniature, the Sun and Moon are within thee, and also the stars.'

This invisible bond between Above and Below is invoked every day around the world in the words of the Lord's Prayer: 'Thy will be done on Earth as it is in Heaven.' This is the key to astrology. By studying the orderly movements of the planetary 'gods' of the solar system, which contains Earth and all its life, the astrologer is studying the conditions of the Above, in order to understand what is going on Below in the individual 'cells of consciousness', such as you and me.

MIND AND MATTER

'In the beginning was the Word.'

THE GOSPEL ACCORDING TO JOHN, OPENING WORDS

Astrology describes the ebb and flow of the primary, divine, creative 'ideas', the 'mind stuff' which shapes and informs all of life and consciousness. For everything in the cosmos is essentially 'mind stuff'. All around us we see matter which is embodying particular ideas. Whether we are looking at a book or a flower, we are looking at the effect of ideas.

We can readily see this with human creativity. From making a dress to building a house, a railway or a computer game, each project starts with an idea in someone's mind. This idea is then translated into some kind of raw material. The materials are always vitally important to the end product, but nevertheless they are secondary to the idea. It is always the idea that in-forms the materials, *and never the other way round.* Destroy every last car in the world and the idea of a car is sufficient to create a new one. No amount of raw materials will ever create a car without the concept. And the creative, in-forming power of ideas equally applies in nature. A rose starts life as an idea written in genetic code. The DNA code then in-forms the raw materials of earth and water and sunshine and, *voila!* You have a rose bush.

The same is true in human lives: the thing we want to make, that finished creation visualized in the mind, is always the last thing to be manifested. Anyone who has done any creative cooking knows that the finest meal, whilst being prepared, generates a great deal of apparent chaos as raw materials are chosen, peeled, chopped, cooked, mixed with herbs, and so on. Creation is messy, and we have to keep our gaze – the mind's eye focused – on that final creation, not to mention the recipe, if we are to believe that all the parts will come together in the right way.

Our personal lives can seem very chaotic, too, if we cannot see the underlying plot. This is what astrology provides – a sense of the plot. The birth chart, as John Addey suggested, is a kind of 'contract with time and space'; and referring to the contract to remind ourselves of the overall game plan can help us to turn chaos into cosmos. Through studying the birth chart, we find out that what feels like chaos is really overemphasis or imbalance in certain areas – too much water (emotionality), too little earth (not enough practicality), an angular Mars (full-steam ahead all the time) – and we then are in a position to make more informed choices which further the plot intelligently. Another analogy is the picture on a packet of seeds: it helps to know ourselves from the horoscope's view of wholeness – are we a delicate fritillary, or a ceanotha which doesn't like too much sun, or a camellia that hates lime, or a hardy honeysuckle that is happy anywhere? By knowing what suits us we can better grow and flourish and actualize our potential.

Astrology is an algebra, a symbolic language which enables us to read the contract, understand the plot, and imaginatively view that unique picture on the packet of seeds which is our life. By engaging imaginatively with the gods within us – the miniature cosmos – we are better equipped to inform the 'matter' of our lives, to grow up and blossom in the way that is best for us. In an essay entitled 'Civilization', Ralph Waldo Emerson (1803–82) expressed a sentiment very close to the idea that astrology encourages. He wrote:

Now that is the wisdom of a man, in every instance of his labour, to hitch his wagon to a star, and see his chore done by the gods themselves. That is the way we are strong, by borrowing the might of the elements … If we can thus ride in Olympian chariots by putting our works in the path of the celestial circuits, we can harness also evil agents, the powers of darkness, and force them to serve against their will the ends of wisdom and virtue.

TIME AND ETERNITY

Time is the flowing image of the Eternal.

PLATO, *TIMAEUS*

Time and space define the field of our existence. They constitute the dual matrix of our astrological calculations. Astrology's perennial questions are: When and where were you born? When and where did this happen? Paradoxically, the astrologer plots out a picture of the cosmos for a particular moment of *space-time* in order to study the pattern of the primary and *eternal* archetypes for the moment.

One image that conveys a sense of the relationship between the temporal and the eternal is the phenomenon of a video tape. The tape contains the whole picture, complete with soundtrack, special effects, the lot. It is all there. But in order to experience the video, we have to unfold it frame by frame at a particular speed. Time is the medium through which we experience the unfolding of what is already all there. The big difference is that the cosmic video (i.e. your life) is unfolding potentialities for each moment. It is for us to express and experience those potentialities. The more conscious and aware we become, the deeper and richer and wiser will be that expression. So yes, there is a strong element of predetermination about this model. But no, it is only the music that is predetermined. How we dance to it, in and through time, is up to us.

SOUL

The birth chart has been described as 'a map of the soul', so a grasp of the concept of soul, or *anima*, is crucial to understanding the position of astrology. Soul is often used interchangeably with spirit; in fact, the two are quite different concepts. To put it simply, spirit is undifferentiated essence, that eternal 'god-stuff' which substands the whole world and everything in it. Opposite to spirit is matter, the temporal stuff which is 'in-formed' by spirit and which we see coming in and out of manifestation throughout our lives, e.g. bodies are born and die, forests grow and then burn down (but yes, as Einstein told us, matter is indestructible – it just changes form). But *between* spirit and matter there is soul, that mysterious principle that brings something to life and personally animates it. The soul is the guardian and channel of our individuality. As already mentioned, the late astrologer John Addey referred to the horoscope as the 'soul's contract with time and space', which emphasizes the uniqueness of each individual life, and that uniqueness is bestowed through soul. The poet Keats spoke of our life on earth as 'the vale of soul-making', which illuminates and makes realizable the precious potential with which we are each born. The birth chart, for those who learn to read it, is an encoded image of every detail of that specific potential. And it is the soul that brings it to life.

The whole world is en-souled; that is, it is alive, growing, dying, and being reborn, all creatures within it being in relationship with and influencing each other. But man is en-souled in a quite unique way, for via the soul he is endowed with the powers and virtues of the whole cosmos. Through soul man forges an individual relationship with the gods and makes a journey through life discovering what he is. Through soul, man has choice and becomes the protagonist in his life drama.

THE PLANETARY GODS

The planetary gods are the main actors in the great mythological stories and in our own life dramas as well. They are the characters that keep the energy and the plot moving along. Each god or planet has distinct attributes, needs and personality. Every chart contains all of them, although the particular way that they appear in each chart is what reveals our uniqueness. The planets of our solar system, with the Sun at the centre, are Mercury, Venus, our Earth, Mars, Jupiter, Saturn, Uranus, Neptune and Pluto. Between Mars and Jupiter is the asteroid belt which includes hundreds of smaller bodies. In addition, there are various other bodies, such as Chiron between Saturn and Uranus, and the Centaurs which circle out beyond Pluto. Some of the planets, such as Earth, also have Moons.

Down the ages the planetary principles (which in Plato's view were 'the first born thoughts of God') have collected many different identities. They are:

- the gods of the different world mythologies;

- the Forms or Ideas of Plato which in-form matter and consciousness;

- the Archetypes of contemporary psychology, the primary templates that shape our psychological growth and relationship with the world;

- the chrono-crators (time-markers) of all historical, philosophical, religious and political movements which inspire, shape and dissolve cultures, nations and empires;

- the hopes and fears of business and economic cycles;

- the movers and changers of the 'flavours of the month' and what is 'in vogue' in the world of art, fashion and the media.

Whether we call them gods or archetypes, forms or ideas, these principles are the fundamental formal causes which weave the tapestry of living Creation out of the passive potentiality of matter. They are the diverse instruments which sound out the cosmic symphony of life in all its harmonic and dissonant subtleties. And they are in us. And the more we come to know the gods in ourselves through understanding our astrological make-up, the more can we make sense of the hopes, the fears, the themes and the events of our life story.

Astrology has no unique claim to understanding these universal formative principles. The patterns of these same ideas are expressed and explored in all the mythologies and theogonies of the world, in fairy tales and dreams. Myth and astrology share the same early origin. Myths express the nature of these archetypal forces in story; astrology maps out their ordered cycles in time. Studying the mythologies of ancient cultures will enrich your understanding of the planetary gods.

Equally, these principles are the basis of all forms of divination by which the underlying processes and purposes of the Cosmos may be approached and glimpsed, such as in numerology, the I Ching, the kabbala and the tarot. Where astrology is unique, however, is in its identification of the way in which the movements of the bodies of the physical solar system mirror, or plot out as on a huge cosmic clock, the moment-to-moment processes of life. Armed with this fundamental insight, astrologers over the centuries have been able to develop a remarkable science and art for studying the creative potential of any moment of space-time, be it past, present or future.

Plato tells us in the *Timaeus* that the planets are 'the instruments of Time', the heavenly bodies whose circular journey around the solar system unfolds the workings of fate like 'clockwork'. A cycle is defined as 'a series that repeats itself', indicating the sense of completeness, as in a circle, as well as a sense of infinity, for once completed the cycle repeats again and again. However, when a planetary cycle repeats, it will never be the same again in relation to the other planetary cycles. Hence, we have a continual unfoldment of cyclical patterns which together weave the loom of Creation.

Every cycle of the heavens and every process of manifestation unfolds itself through a number of distinct phases, each with its own characteristics. This archetypal process was encapsulated by early astrologers in the cycle of the zodiac, or literally the 'circle of the animals', from the Greek zoon, as in a zoo.

This cycle describes twelve distinct phases of any cycle. Each phase is given a different 'sign', usually an evocative animal symbol (see Chapter 6) that encapsulates and acts as an aide memoire to the essential meaning of that phase. As such this zodiacal process was projected on to the pattern of the stars, the constellations, to mark out the phases of the primary cycle in 'the Above'. This sequence of signs was probably first used to describe the cycle of the seasons, which followed the apparent annual movement of the Sun around the Earth. This cycle, measured from the Spring equinox or First Point of Aries, is still the primary circle used by astronomers.

So that when an astrologer is asked 'what sign are you?' she might answer 'I have the Sun in Capricorn, the Moon, Mid-Heaven, Venus and Jupiter all in Aquarius and Gemini rising'. This identifies the phases of this universal cycle that are being emphasized by each the different dimensions of the individual.

Apart from the zodiac which describes the basic cycle of seasonal manifestation, each fixed star has its own cycle of rising and culminating. The times in the annual cycle at which specific fixed stars, such as Sirius, rose and set just before or after the Sun were considered very important. The nature and significance of each star was studied in great detail, though this is beyond the scope of this book.

The main focus of astrological study focused upon the wandering stars, the planetary gods. Each planet has its own specific cycle. Indeed all our normally used time frames are related to planetary cycles:

- a day is the time it takes for the Earth to rotate on its axis;

- a week is a quarter of a lunar cycle;

- a month is a Moonth, or the time from one New Moon to the next;

- a year is the time it takes for the Earth to go around the Sun.

Even if you are not aware of the association, you are already familiar with some of the principles of astrology. The seven days of the week, which are part of the very foundation of the way the whole world organizes its time, are named after the seven planets known to the ancient world:

- Sun-day, the day of the Sun

- Mon-day, the day of the Moon

- Tuesday, – in French *Mar-di* – the day of Mars

- Wednesday – in French *Mercre-di* – the day of Mercury

- Thursday – in French *Jeu-di* – the day of Jove or Jupiter

- Friday – in French *Vendre-di* – the day of Venus

- Saturday – the day of Saturn

The English names are the Teutonic equivalents of the same gods.

The birth chart appears to be a static 'thing' that endures for a lifetime, but the cycles of the planets unfold the chart's potential. A planet returns to its original position at birth when it completes a cycle, although the planets complete their journey around the zodiac in different periods of time. Jupiter's cycle, which unfolds our search for meaning and expansion, is about 12 years long. Saturn's cycle takes about 29 years to complete. The famous Saturn Return is a time of growing up, taking responsibility, and making commitments. The second Saturn Return, which occurs at the age of 58, takes us into the last chapter of life when we must examine what our life has achieved and when we must face the inevitability of our death. The Uranus cycle is 84 years long. During the half-way point of this planet's journey around the zodiac, at the age of about 40 (give or take a few years due to orbital eccentricity), people have their mid-life crisis when repressed desires erupt to bring either a chaotic or newly creative period. In a very dramatic way, life may never seem the same after the Uranus opposition.

In a sense, life is never the same after any of the planets complete their cycles, and this is because the chart has unfolded more of its potentialities, during which time choices have been made, directions have been taken, doors have been opened – and closed.

LEVELS OF EXPRESSION

It is important to recognize that the planetary archetypes express themselves in different ways throughout all levels of cosmic and human life. To take an example, the planet Mars will express its assertive, potent, territorial, separative, propelling nature:

- in the physical world as heat, energy, fire, explosions;

- in the plant world as thorns, poisons, acids, stinging species such as nettles;

- in the animal kingdom as territoriality, predatory activity, the mating instinct;

- in the body as the immune system, and also in the occurrence of accidents, cuts, bruises, inflammation, and fever in the body which harm – and which activate the immune system;

- at an emotional level as anger, retaliation – saying 'no'

- at the level of will as self-assertion, competitiveness, the will to win, courage;

- at the level of intellect as singularity, cutting out superfluous thought, emphasizing, and decisive communication;

- at the mystical level as the sword of truth.

These principles, gods, archetypes and myths show and express themselves at every level. In the physical world they can be detected at work in the ever-changing climate and the occurrence of storms, floods, earthquakes, natural disasters. In the individual, they can be observed in life themes and in the output of one's work. For example, Queen Elizabeth, with Saturn exactly conjunct the uppermost point of her chart (status, public responsibility), has stood for tradition and the supreme rule of monarchy. The comedian Spike Milligan's life, with Uranus exactly rising in Aquarius, has expressed the opposite: eccentricity, anarchic humour, poking fun at the class system, rules and bogus certainty. As you become more familiar with the planetary archetypes, you can begin to see the body of the cosmos and the body of man alive and expressing the interplay of all these energies, as in a great mythological drama.

NUMBER

The ancients spoke of the Creator as the Great Geometrician. This is because the greatest minds in all the ancient cultures observed that all living entities developed, or emerged from potential into manifestation, through an ordered, logical and numerical process. Pythagoras was the first to develop the science of number to a sophisticated level. He and his followers learned to think in numbers, to reflect upon realities in their progressive states. And to these progressive states they gave the names of numbers.

The Pythagoreans believed that the first 10 numbers contained the secret of all things, and that each of the first decade of numbers was a primary creative principle in the Cosmos, indeed a God.

Number in the deepest sense relates to the creative processes of the cosmos. With regards to the birth, flowering, and death of any entity, number describes the archetypal relationship between part and whole.

Archetypal number is at the heart of astrology. We come to understand 'two-ness' in the two-fold division of positive and negative signs, in the ascendant (self)—descendant (other) axis,

which divides the chart into an upper horizon section (more extrovert) and lower horizon section (more introvert). We grapple with 'three-ness' in the three modes of expression – cardinal, fixed and mutable; and with 'four-ness' in the four elements – fire, earth, air, water – and also in the four angles of the chart, ascendant (east), descendant (west), midheaven (south), and immum coeli (north). The 12 signs of the zodiac are made up of the three modes and four elements. And the unfolding cycles of the planets express themselves through number in the aspects. The study of astrology is the study of the rhythms of the universe as they relate to the individual, and *rhythm is number*. From this point of view, astrology connects us to the inner reality of things, if we are sufficiently sensitive to perceive the mystery unfolding before our very eyes.

FATE

Astrology has always had a reputation for encouraging a sense of determinism and predestination. People often express apprehension about looking into astrology, for they are frightened they will learn what fate awaits them. The I Ching tells us that the destinies of men are subject to immutable laws that must fulfil themselves, but that man has the power to shape his fate 'according as his *behaviour* exposes him to the influence of benevolent or destructive forces'. But notice our emphasis of the word 'behaviour'. We can use the knowledge of ourselves we gain from astrology, and simply from our experience of life, to act in accord with a more desirable outcome. To benefit from astrological insights, one must exert effort. That is where the real free will lies. (As Schopenhauer said, 'We may have free will, but not the will to use it.') A person having Saturn transit their Sun will know that it is not a time to take risks or to try to expand in adventurous directions, but rather a time to consolidate one's material and professional position, a time to carry current responsibilities successfully.

Certain parameters are fixed in life. That is the nature of reality, for man cannot live in a vacuum. The contract with time and space is signed and sealed at birth; the parents and family we were born to and the society and historical period in which we gain our identity cannot be changed; the life drama we have chosen is ready to be played. But within the matrix of our given life parameters, we have the freedom to make choices. It is the unique combination of fate and free will that provides the psychic soil out of which we grow and live our lives. That same psychic soil grows heroes and heroines. In fact, man is free only in his mind, his inner attitude. Changes in fate are made according to inner attitude – that is what determines the wisdom of our choices, and ultimately our fate.

THE USES
OF ASTROLOGY

Astrology is Astronomy brought down to earth and applied to
the affairs of man.

RALPH WALDO EMERSON

A strology is best known for its power to describe character and for its ability to 'look into the future'. These
are certainly two important applications. However, the
basic principles of astrology can be applied to almost every
area of life. In this chapter we will look at what to expect when
consulting an astrologer and some of the many and diverse
areas in which astrology can be applied to obtain a fresh perspective and dynamic understanding of life.

CONSULTING AN ASTROLOGER –
WHAT TO EXPECT

Some useful addresses and web sites for obtaining details of
qualified astrologers, in Britain and around the world, can be
found on pages 247–252.

Most astrologers in the English-speaking world work with
western tropical astrology, as taught in this book, although
there is now a growing number of Vedic astrologers in the West

who practise sidereal astrology following the ancient Hindu tradition. The work of this rich tradition is beyond the scope of this book.

As astrology tends to be a subject which, like psychology, benefits enormously from life experience, few astrologers qualify before their Saturn Return, when they are about 30 years old. About 80 to 90 per cent of astrology students on most courses are women and probably 80 per cent of practitioners at the present time are females. This is probably because women usually have better access to the right-brain functions associated with poetry, imagination, the metaphorical and the symbolic, and a natural interest in people and their psychology. These are essential qualities for working fully and effectively with astrology. An increasing number of astrologers will also have some kind of additional training in counselling.

Like doctors, astrologers usually undergo broad training, which familiarizes them with most branches of astrology. Then, when the astrologer sets up in practice, she will tend to specialize in one particular area, and will probably undertake additional training. The great majority of practitioners now work in the area of psychological astrology and character analysis. Most psychological astrologers will also undertake work on chart comparison and relationships, including parent–child relationships and family dynamics in general.

Astrologers usually work by personal consultation, usually from an office within their own home and sometimes in alternative health centres. Very few astrologers are sufficiently affluent to have their own secretary or receptionist, so the consultation is normally booked directly with the astrologer herself, who will take the preliminary details and possibly some case history.

THE ESSENTIAL INFORMATION

The information required by all astrologers is the date, time and place of birth. The time of birth is essential, but this can be problematic as in Britain the time is only recorded on the birth certificate in Scotland, except in the case of multiple births. If you were born in a hospital or a nursing home your time of birth will be on your original birth records, which the authorities are obliged to keep until you are 21. After that your records may be less readily accessible or even destroyed.

Astrologers vary a lot as to whether they want to take a detailed case history before the consultation. Some astrologers prefer to work 'blind', allowing the chart to speak for itself in terms of its pure potential. They will then relate that potential to the actual life history later in the consultation. Most astrologers will ask you the reason for the consultation and any special issues that you would like them to consider.

THE CONSULTATION

A typical first consultation or reading of a natal chart with an astrologer will last between 90 minutes and two hours, and sometimes longer. Prior to your arrival, the astrologer will probably have spent at least an hour preparing your natal chart, usually with the help of a computer, looking at current trends and probably making notes. If it is a first consultation the astrologer may well have prepared the chart several days earlier and have had it mulling over in the back of her mind for some while.

When it is not possible to meet in person, some astrologers work very effectively by phone. Some will also supply a reading dictated on to a cassette. A few astrologers will provide written reports. These, however, are very costly as a full written report would be unlikely to take less than one full day to prepare and write up.

Fees vary considerably. A first consultation is unlikely to cost less than £50 with a follow-up hourly rate of £20. A top astrologer in London will charge at least £40 per hour which, allowing for preparation time, will mean that the first consultation could be about £90 or £100.

CHARACTER ANALYSIS

At the simplest level, an astrologer can interpret your horoscope as a pattern of character traits, aptitudes, strengths and weaknesses. This approach is purely descriptive, the astrologer attempting to sketch out a personality profile in words and images. If you have a lot of fire in your chart and a strong ninth house, you will be seen as impulsive, energetic, intuitive, idealistic and mentally adventurous. If you have a strongly placed Saturn in the first house as well, you will also be described as serious, self-doubting, ponderous, but reliable and conscientious too. These and other contrasting features of your character will be identified, together with the inner tensions and creative potential they involve. It will then be up to you to go away and draw your own conclusions.

PSYCHOLOGICAL ASTROLOGY

An astrological consultation will reveal valuable insights about your personality and the dilemmas you experience in life, but it will not change deep-seated behaviour patterns or heal psychological wounds overnight. However, since we humans are blessed with the faculty of self-reflection, we can choose to go beyond a mere description of our character and actually engage with this knowledge in a deeper way. If you find that the beauty of this language really speaks to you, astrology becomes a kind of wisdom path which can lead to empowerment and desired life changes. This takes time, commitment, and the development of self-analysis.

Some people are natural self-analysers. Others will benefit immeasurably from the experience of psychotherapy where someone else analyses and, over time, teaches you to self-analyse. Add astrology to this activity and you suddenly have a much more powerful experience of understanding what is going on. In this way, astrological insights can help us work through negative conditionings and to see that when it comes to forming our inner attitude, there is a choice.

When the astrologer moves from giving descriptions of personality to relating energies in the chart to the actual personal experience of the individual, the astrologer is also acting as a counsellor. Increasingly now, astrologers undergo some kind of therapeutic training which enables them to listen effectively and to manage the emotional responses of clients, rather than just impart information. If you wish to work more deeply with astrology as a tool for self-awareness, it is important that the astrologer you choose has experience and training in counselling. The Faculty of Astrological Studies offers a two-year Counselling Within Astrology course, and the Centre for Psychological Astrology offers a broad base of knowledge in psychological theory and requires students to be in individual therapy for a minimum of one year. A list of qualified astrologers is available through the Faculty of Astrological Studies and the Association for Professional Astrologers (see Astrological Resources, page 247).

Some astrologers are beginning to work with astrology as a framework for longer-term therapeutic work. C.G. Jung's daughter, Frau Gret Baumann Jung, was a great pioneer of this approach. Each of her therapeutic clients was given an introductory book on astrology and asked to study the basic principles so as to be able to work within that archetypal frame-work. She believed that the value of inner work was greatly enhanced by astrological symbolism, and that it encouraged within her clients both a sense of responsibility and a desire for self-knowledge. Astrology's ability to enrich the meaning-making process makes it a central tool for all people who seek a greater experience of freedom in their lives.

LIFE TRENDS – FORECASTING THE FUTURE

What will happen to us? What is our destiny? Astrology can never answer these questions in absolute terms. The astrologer looking at a chart cannot see 'events' and people written on it. The astrologer sees in a chart combinations of energy and patterns of ideas which experience has shown are likely to manifest in certain ways. By studying the chart it is possible to see the kinds of issues that are likely to arise in a person's life. If the astrologer knows how an individual has responded to certain kinds of patterns in the past, and also knows the current circumstances, it becomes more possible to make reasonably reliable inferences about the way that things may develop.

By the same measure, knowing the kind of energies which will be to the fore at a particular time, the astrologer will suggest ways in which they can be most constructively be directed. Thus planetary patterns which an astrology textbook might associate with the breakdown of a relationship may in practice express themselves as a 'breakthrough' which transforms rather than breaks the existing relationship. Ultimately, how the chart expresses itself is not preordained but a matter of individual consciousness and choice.

Almost everyone who decides to consult an astrologer wants to know what will happen to them. But destiny is, in fact, simply

another expression of character. To the astrologer, they are one and the same thing. To take a simple example, a person with the planet Jupiter prominent will tend to be optimistic. Because he is cheerful, people will like him. This jovial type will tend to see the opportunities in any situation and people will be inclined to help. Thus he appears to be 'lucky' as ever-new vistas open up for him. By contrast, someone with Saturn in a dominant position at birth will be inclined to pessimism. The saturnine type will focus on life's problems and may spend much time and energy defending against 'what may happen' and in becoming self-reliant. In the longer run, the eternal optimist may start too many ventures and finish none of them, take too many risks and waste his resources. By contrast, Saturn's disciple, who has carefully put aside resources for a rainy day, and who has finished each project as it comes along, may well end up as a person of substance who has made a real tangible difference to the world. In each case, however, character has led the way and an astrologer merely reads the signatures of character and its implications.

Astrology cannot 'foretell the future' as such. It can, however, look at the qualities of a particular period and, like a weather forecaster, make intelligent conjectures about the kind of issues we are likely to be facing.

RELATIONSHIPS

Relationships make up a crucially important part of most people's lives. Indeed, the world's literature, film and media industry, not to mention the work of psychotherapists and psychiatrists, would shrivel to almost nothing without the challenge of human relationships. So, not surprisingly, there is a whole branch of astrology devoted to the study of the way people are likely to get on with each other.

Known as 'synastry' (literally 'combined stars'), this branch of astrology provides a powerful means of studying the dynamics which are created in all kinds of relationships, be it between lovers, teacher and pupil, business partners, parent and child, and so on.

By comparing and combining the different birth charts, the astrologer can provide valuable insights about the way in which people are likely to get on with each other and the kind of dynamics which will probably emerge in the relationship.

This type of comparison goes way beyond the grossly over-simplified sun sign 'compatibility' charts, beloved of popular articles on astrology. Whilst different sun signs can be more or less compatible with one another, the comparison of charts is much more complex. In fact, a compatibility of moon signs is usually much more important than sun signs for a long-term relationship of any kind. Likewise, the idea that different astrological types will have different kinds of relationships is essentially sound.

Whether it is our relationship with a lover or a colleague, with our parents, our brothers and sisters, with friends, employers, fellow workers, our own children or with society at large, astrology will have something to say. The principles of astrology can be used to understand the kinds of things we will seek in a relationship and the kinds of issues that relationships are likely to bring up for us.

We can also learn why different relationships bring out different sides of our personality, why we feel upbeat and optimistic with some people and down or awkward with others.

VOCATIONAL GUIDANCE

Astrology can be an invaluable adjunct to helping decide the kind of work or career someone might find most suitable and rewarding in relation to their innate skills. The birth chart cannot say that someone will be a musician or a social worker or an accountant. It can, however, indicate that, say, music or the care of others, or the effective and creative handling of resources, are likely to be things they will enjoy and at which they have a good chance of finding personal satisfaction and success.

Equally, the birth chart can indicate areas of work and finances which are more likely to bring problems or upsets. The individual in whose chart Uranus features strongly may find it difficult to work in a subservient position and find themselves constantly at loggerheads with authority figures. The strongly Neptunian type may be drawn by their deeply compassionate nature to helping others, yet find it difficult to look after themselves and protect their own boundaries and resources.

By drawing out and clarifying different talents and aptitudes, the astrologer can help the individual to obtain a larger picture of the kind of work and career they are likely to find really satisfying, and in which they will feel motivated to work hard to succeed. Or, in the case of workaholics who are determined to make life tough for themselves, astrology may help to identify those areas where they may benefit without so much stress and strain.

MEDICAL MATTERS

In the ancient world and until the end of the 16th century, astrology was always a central part of a doctor's university training and medical practice. If you studied medicine you automatically learned astrology as a means of helping you with both diagnosis and prognosis. Rightly so, for the affinity between each part of the body and the planets and signs of the zodiac can give a medically trained astrologer invaluable clues as to underlying tensions and stresses and the weak areas of the body where problems are likely to manifest.

By studying the chart of an individual and the chart of the moment when he or she was taken ill, or took to their bed, the astrologer can make deductions as to the kinds of issues that are likely to be involved in the illness and the likely critical points in the days ahead. Likewise an astrologer with a medical background and training can use the birth chart to help better understand the kinds of physical problems an individual may experience, the kinds of precautionary and dietary measures to take, and the kinds of therapy that may be most beneficial to them.

However, no one without some kind of medical training should attempt to use the birth chart in this way. Just as an ill-informed reading of a medical encyclopaedia can quickly make one believe that one has typhoid fever, multiple sclerosis and Alzheimer's, so too can novice astrologers immediately believe the medical worst of difficult patterns in a chart, or of difficult times ahead for themselves and their nearest and dearest.

All major transits and progressions to sensitive points in the natal chart can express themselves in part through the body. The transits of Saturn, Chiron and Neptune are particularly prone to express themselves in physical terms.

An astrologer with a knowledge of medicine can use astrology to understand the processes going on within an individual at both a psychological and a physical level. For example, someone with a prominent but poorly integrated Mars in their chart is likely both to be prone to unnecessarily forceful, aggressive behaviour and to be accident-prone and run fevers.

CHOOSING THE BEST TIME

To everything there is a season
And a time to every purpose under the heavens

ECCLESIASTES 3

If you want to launch a boat it is usually simpler to wait for the tide to come in and float the boat off the shore than to push the boat down the beach and across the shingle. Astrology can be used to elect – that is choose – the optimum time to start any particular project. Hence this branch of astrology is technically known as 'electional astrology'. The principles of electional astrology can be applied to any enterprise that has a definable starting moment.

Choosing the right time for undertakings has always been a major role for the astrologer. It is now public knowledge that President Ronald Reagan never made any major initiative without optimizing the chances of success by getting the timing right. From his first inauguration as Governor of California to his declarations for the US Presidency, none of the major decisions in his life were taken without astrological advice. As Reagan's aide Donald Regan testifies in his autobiography, the time of the signing of the Test Ban Treaty with Gorbachov was arranged to chime in with the heavens, rather than procedural convenience, much to the chagrin of the military.

As a result, someone who was generally considered to be a relatively simple soul managed to win almost every contest he entered, and to succeed in putting bills through Congress despite being head of a minority Government.

MARRIAGE

Getting married is a major venture for anyone, and if you have a choice, it makes good sense to plan the timing of this event.

the chances of mutual understanding and a long-lasting and happy bond. Indeed, throughout the Indian sub-continent and much of Asia, few couples will get married without first ensuring that the day is a propitious one for them. In this case the astrologer will look at the possible dates and see:

- which dates and times yield the most harmonious charts;

- the relationship between the chart and the charts of the bride and groom.

Likewise if success is going to hinge upon the wellbeing of one or two key people, then it is a good idea to choose a time which will bring out the best in them and minimize the sense of stress and strain.

BUSINESS PROJECTS

The time to start any particular project will depend both on the nature of the work being undertaken and the chart of the people most closely involved with it. If you are starting a project you want to develop quickly and to catch the public eye, you will need to choose a different kind of time from a project which requires plenty of peace and quiet and a slow, steady approach.

By analogy, if you are arranging a mail-out and want to optimize the chances of it going smoothly and your communication being read, it is a good idea to ensure that Mercury, planet of communication, and the Moon, which rules the mood of the moment, are well placed. The kind of placement the astrologer will choose will be dependent upon the kind of mail involved. If the desire is to encourage a sense of optimism and wellbeing the astrologer will want to choose a different kind of climate to

PRINCIPLES OF ASTROLOGY

one which is suggesting that people enrol on a course of study, or purchase life insurance.

No matter how good the starting chart for a venture, it cannot of itself make up for lack of sound preparation and good management.

CHOOSING THE BEST PLACE

We are each born at a particular place on Earth, and our birth chart is normally calculated for that place. But there is a sense in which each one of us is also incarnated on to the Earth as a whole, as part of the world soul. This may sound like a poetic flight of fancy. In practice, this is found to be an extremely valuable reality. For example, we may have been born in Britain at midnight, placing our sun in the fourth house (see Chapter 7), the position of a home-loving individual who tends to a private rather than a public life. If we move to the other side of the world to New Zealand, where it would have been midday when we were born, and recalculate our chart for Wellington, say, we will find the Sun will be in the tenth house, of public affairs and personal career achievement. Suddenly, from having been a relatively retiring, domestic individual, we are likely to find ourselves out in the limelight, perhaps seeking public office and playing a more authoritative role within the community. And for everyone there will be places in the world where the Sun comes to the fore, and places where it can hide away and obtain some peace and quiet. In short, there are different places where different faces of the soul can thrive.

Such Relocation Charts, as they are called, have been known about since early this century. If you were trying to decide whether to go to Malaga or Corfu for your holidays you could relocate your chart to each place to see what aspects of your chart are brought to the fore at each resort. It would then be possible to choose the place that looked more likely to bring out the kind of energies you would find enjoyable for a holiday.

However, you may be a businessman or woman and want to know which areas of the world are likely to be especially advantageous for you or for your company's products. To calculate a chart for every major city of the world would be out of the question. Happily, with the advent of the computer, the brilliant American astrologer Jim Lewis was able to develop a program, known as Astro*Carto*Graphy, which plots the positions of the planets at the time of birth on to a map of the world. This, and other imitation astro-locality programmes, enables the astrologer to identify immediately where in the world different planetary energies will come to the fore.

Using astro-locality techniques, it is possible to find parts of the world that will assist in one's enterprises and self-knowledge, both generally and at particular times in your life. However, such methods need to be used with caution. If your birth chart shows that you have a strong but problematic Jupiter, which makes for joviality but also for over-optimism and extravagance, it may not be advisable to go rushing off somewhere where you can practise your generosity to the utmost! That said, the use of astro-locality can reach parts of your personality and potential that other methods cannot. If a change of scene is as good as a rest, astro-locality can be invaluable in helping us choose the optimum scene.

JUDGING THE MOMENT

Someone may already have decided that they are going to start a particular course, or go on holiday at a particular time, or have got married. There may be little choice in the matter. In such cases the astrologer can highlight the main kinds of issues

that are likely to arise and point out where the greatest potential and problems are likely to be.

Many astrologers look at the chart for the time that a client first contacts them and the time of the first appointment. Such charts can be highly revealing of the main issues concerning the client. So, too, a chart set for a 'first meeting' can be extremely revealing of the significance and future course of the relationship. The late poet laureate, Ted Hughes, who had a good working knowledge of astrology, described the astrological factors surrounding his meeting with Sylvia Plath in his poem 'St Bartolph's' in *Birthday Letters* and concluded:

> That day the solar system married us
> Whether we knew it or not.

ASKING QUESTIONS – HORARY

One of the simplest and richest forms of astrology is the specialist area of 'horary' astrology which is based on the chart for the 'hora' or 'hour' – the time a pressing question is asked, or when it is received by the astrologer. In recent years a growing number of astrologers have begun to specialize in this ancient type of astrology. It can be very valuable in throwing light on specific issues, such as 'Should I take the job?'. Such a question may have deep psychological as well as practical implications. A study of an horary chart for such a question can be expected to reveal something about the background to the question and the issues involved, practical information about the timing, and, in the hands of a psychological horary practitioner, something of the larger personal issues implied in the question.

This is based on the idea that the moment when someone feels sufficiently moved to contact an astrologer with a pressing question will be a moment which will in itself reflect the nature

of that question. This is often the case to a striking degree. In 59
fact, in India, anyone regularly consulting an astrologer will
expect the astrologer to know what they are calling about from
the chart for the moment of their enquiry.

ASTROLOGY AND LITERATURE

All great writing, be it in the form of a novel, drama or poetry,
touches on an archetypal level of understanding of people and
life. This is why mythology and such archetypal studies as
astrology, kabbala and tarot have always had a deep fascination
for artists of all kinds. Some of the great literary giants of the
past and of this century have drawn their insight, imagery and
inspiration from astrology. In the medieval world, Chaucer and
Dante; in the Renaissance, Marcilio Ficino and Shakespeare; in
this century such giants as James Joyce, W.B. Yeats, André Breton, Henry Miller and Herman Hesse. Amongst contemporary
writers, Lindsay Clarke and the late poet laureate Ted Hughes
acknowledge the power of the starry archetypal elixir.

Because astrology speaks so graphically of the inner motiva-
tions, conflicts and dynamics within the human psyche, it is an
admirable tool for penetrating into the mind of the writer and
can be used very effectively as an instrument for literary criticism and understanding. We know of more than one literary
doctorate and several biographies which have drawn, often
unacknowledged, on astrology for their insights into the creative personality of their subjects. Indeed it could be said that
anyone engaged in biographical studies who ignores the astrological dimension is denying themselves a rich blueprint of that
person's life.

THE ASTROLOGY OF WORLD AFFAIRS – MUNDANE ASTROLOGY

This is the most ancient use of astrology. Its name comes from the Latin *mundus*, meaning the world. It studies how the dominant planetary sign positions and patterns are likely to express themselves in world cultural, economic and political affairs. By studying the birth chart (or charts) of a nation it is possible to assess the way in which the prevailing astrological climate is likely to affect the *Zeitgeist*, the spirit of the time. There are probably no full-time mundane astrologers at present. However, an increasing number of astrologers are familiar with interpreting charts for the kinds of trends and events that are likely in any period. Mundane astrology can provide insights into current affairs and can make informed forecasts about future political and economic trends for the world as a whole and for individual nations.

ASTRO-ECONOMICS

This is a specialist area of mundane astrology which has major implications for international economic planning. Astro-economics studies the relationship between astrological cycles and such things as the business cycle, the ebb and flow of stock markets, commodity prices, currency fluctuations and business confidence. Certain planetary cycles are especially strong movers of markets. Most notably, the 20-year cycle of Jupiter and Saturn, and its 10-year half-cycle, seems to regulate the alternations of optimism (greed) and pessimism (fear) of the markets.

The importance of the Jupiter–Saturn cycle has been independently noted and verified by non-astrologers such as the American economist Clifford Matlock, and most recently by the

Cambridge economist Dr Hamish Watson. The triple Jupiter–Saturn cycle of 60 years marks major longer-term shifts in economic confidence. The sixth part of this cycle, the 3.33-year cycle, marks out the main features of the shorter 40-month business cycle.

Each of the planetary cycles has its own particular area of resonance. So, for example, the *c.* 12-year Jupiter–Uranus cycle marks major phases in technological innovation whilst the *c.* 40-year Saturn–Uranus cycle is significant for the harnessing of technology and plays an important part in the timing of shifts in the US stock market in particular. The 12-year Jupiter–Neptune cycle is found to be related to inflation and periods of euphoria in the markets. The *c.* 2-year cycles of Mars with Jupiter and Saturn mark out the intermediate ebbs and flows within the cycle of optimistic and pessimistic business sentiment.

Not all markets respond equally strongly to the same cycles, or necessarily in the same way. So, for example, there will be differences between emerging markets and mature markets, between those economies which are strongly focused on primary materials and those that are focused on services industries or high technology.

FINANCIAL INVESTMENT AND SPECULATION

A growing number of stock, commodity and currency traders use astrological indicators to help guide their understanding of the timing of likely trends in the market and changes in individual stock prices. Astrologers who specialize in this area can often identify key days when the market is likely to make dramatic moves or major reversals. Indeed, it is sometimes possible to pin down the precise hour and even minute when a particular market is likely to turn. Equally, it is often possible to indicate when changes will occur in particular sectors of the

market or when specific shares are likely to become the focus of attention.

This type of information ought to make astrologers wealthy. However, like every other application of astrology, it is not enough to know the timing. It is also important to have an intimate understanding of the way markets work and the trading experience and the financial discipline to know when to stay with one's judgement and when to cut one's losses. Few astrologers have these market skills. When an individual has combined these skills, as in the case of 'the guru of Wall Street', the late W.D. Gann, the result can be phenomenal.

Another key use of financial astrology is evaluating the prospects of individual businesses from the chart for the incorporation of the company. A study of such charts can identify periods of growth, setbacks, tensions and possible mergers and takeovers. Likewise, an astrologer who specializes in this area can evaluate the stock prospects of a quoted company from a chart set for the time of its first trade on the stock market.

BUSINESS ASTROLOGY

Astrologers are increasingly being used within companies to help with such matters as long-term planning, choosing times to launch products, open branch offices, enter into negotiations, arrange mergers and takeovers, assess competitors, help with personnel selection and generally give another perspective on business decisions.

Of particular value to businesses with an international exposure is the ability of astrology to give insights into areas of the world which are likely to be especially beneficial to them, and to provide some indication of the likely stability or otherwise of emerging nations and markets.

ASTRO-DRAMA AND EXPERIENTIAL ASTROLOGY

We are all constantly expressing our charts in endless ways on many different levels. But when we come to try and understand it with an astrologer in order to work more effectively with our potential, he or she will of necessity have to translate it into ideas and words and images. Whilst this can give us a valuable intellectual understanding of the dynamics within us, it cannot fully evoke the experience. Astro-drama and 'Experiential Astrology' workshops are a means of directly experiencing the patterns of one's life as revealed in the birth chart through acting them out with other people. For some people the experience of actually engaging in a drama with other people the tensions and contradictions of, say, Sun opposite Neptune (the principle of individual self-hood in opposition to the principle of transcendent, collective unity), can be deeply revealing and healing in a way that no amount of intellectual discussion can achieve.

The patterns of the birth chart can also be deliberately explored through painting, music and dance. Such non-verbal approaches bring about another level of understanding which, through by-passing the intellect, reach directly into an emotional and physical level of consciousness. This can at times produce responses that reach down to the individual cells of the body. In this way, habitual patterns of energy which are blocking self-development can begin to be re-expressed in more constructive ways.

ASTROLOGY AND MAGIC

In the East there is a long tradition of working with astrological patterns through appropriate prayers, mantras, rituals, the use of gem stones, amulets and appropriate dietary considerations. This was also common in the West in the Middle Ages as a major branch of ritual magic and alchemy. The great Renaissance philosopher Marsilio Ficino advised working with astrological 'magic' to better balance the birth chart. For example, if you are having problems with the Mars principle of self-assertion, then by making an especial effort to honour Mars by wearing red, eating hot and spicy food and generally identifying with the principle, he becomes your friend rather than your enemy.

ASTROLOGY AND MYSTICAL CONTEMPLATION

It is possible to think and work with astrology as though it were an impersonal, mechanical process like heat or light, electricity or gravity. Yet the experience of anyone who has been working with astrology for any length of time is that it does not obey precisely measurable 'laws'. Even in those areas where astrology appears for a while to be most reliable and mechanical, as in the actions of the stock market, planetary processes have a habit of suddenly finding alternative, but symbolically appropriate, forms of expression. The more one watches the astrological at work in individuals, in companies and countries and the daily news, the more one is aware that these cyclical processes, whilst predictable in terms of timing, have a mind of their own as regards expression. One is, as it were, watching the ebb and flow of consciousness within the world.

For example, the events of 1989, under the Saturn–Neptune conjunction, as the old order (Saturn) dissolved (Neptune) were as much music, art and poetry as mechanics. The rigidities of apartheid evaporated in South Africa. The Berlin Wall crumbled. The monolithic Soviet Union disappeared almost overnight. Whilst individuals, such as Mikhail Gorbachev and Václav Havel, were involved in these events, such individuals appear to the astrologer as spokespersons for these Ideas of History. The Ideas were flowing through every cell of consciousness in the collective, creating a momentum to which the world leaders responded.

So likewise, during late 1997 through into 1999, as Saturn forms its square phase to Neptune, the world has witnessed a crisis in 'the new economic order' that the West believed it had established in 1989. The heavens once again indicate to the world that it is not adequately honouring both Saturn and Neptune. The flow of international speculative capital (Neptune) has been destroying local economies (Saturn) and ignoring the need to control (Saturn) speculative greed (Neptune).

Plato said that 'the true philosopher is a spectator of Time and Eternity'. The astrologer, by contemplating the instruments of time, the planetary movements, is enabled to become a witness to the workings of the Eternal Archetypes in her own life and the life of family, friends and the famous. Everywhere the astrologer looks she is, through her science and art, enabled to glimpse ever deeper levels of meaning and purpose behind the seeming tragedies, trivialities and triumphs of daily life.

The work of the astrologer, both personally and with clients, is to endeavour to bring an awareness and understanding of these processes at work within the individual soul and the collective. Ideally, this work can enable us to live a life of increasingly conscious resonance with the pattern of living Ideas portrayed in our chart. For, as Plato points out:

By a life in conformity with the Ideal, a light, as from a fire, is enkindled in the Soul and there its self nourishes itself.

The more we are in tune with our inner nature, the more alive we become. This goal is summarized by the great fifth-century Neo-Platonic philosopher and astrologer Proclus in his *The Theology of Plato* in what could be considered to be the astrologers' credo and goal:

> We must say therefore, that there are divine dances ... the dance of the Gods ... and that of divine souls ... the revolution of the celestial divinities, viz. of the seven planets ... And the whole life of a philosopher is a dance. Who then are those that honour the Goddess in the dance? Not those who dance well, but those who live well through the whole of their present existence, elegantly arranging their life, and dancing in symphony with the universe.

In the following chapters we will be focusing on natal astrology. However, the principles of this 'algebra of life' are generally applicable to each of the other branches discussed in this chapter. The planets, signs and houses retain their same essential meanings, as do the aspects.

THE PLANETARY GODS

We have an entire sky within us, our fiery strength and heavenly origin: Luna which symbolizes the continuous motion of soul and body, Mars speed and Saturn slowness, the Sun God, Jupiter law, Mercury reason, and Venus humanity.

MARSILIO FICINO

ods? Ideas? Archetypes? Principles? Deciding what we call the intelligent processes in the cosmos, represented by the physical bodies and orbits of the planets, will depend upon our background and mindset. The authors feel that exploring the planets as 'gods' is appropriate because:

- the term conveys that the first principles of astrology are living, purposeful processes with 'minds of their own';

- 'gods' connects us immediately to mythology, the richest source of knowledge we have about these archetypal forces which are present in all people;

- the term implies that the universe, rather than being an inanimate, mechanical 'thing', is alive, interconnected, and pulsating with energy, stories, and meaning;

- it conveys that each of us is also a living microcosmos, also bursting with stories and purposes;

- it reminds us that however much we understand about life, she remains a mystery, and that ultimately 'we propose, but the gods dispose'.

The solar system is a unitive, integral whole, each planet being an essential part of that whole. Therefore, each planet or 'god' plays its unique role within the system; each planet represents a particular function in relation to the whole. The word 'planet' derives from the Greek meaning 'wanderer', and in ancient times they were the mysterious wanderers of the night sky. But they were not wandering just anywhere; it was discovered that they were headed in a purposeful direction, one which mapped out a very definite cycle related to every other cycle within the solar system. Likewise for human beings, the planets represent parts or functions of the whole psyche, each having its own essential energy and purpose, and forming the focus of a different 'side' or 'sub-personality' within us. The planetary model of the psyche evinces its rich complexity, and allows us to identify and learn to value all the different parts of ourselves. Every birth chart features all 10 astrological 'gods', which represent the following functions:

SUN	☉	self-integration, vitality, conscious authority
MOON	☽	unconscious emotional response, rhythm, receptivity
MERCURY	☿	communication, mental faculties
VENUS	♀	sociability, love, beauty
MARS	♂	self-assertion, competition
JUPITER	♃	expansion, opportunity, search for meaning
SATURN	♄	structure, limitation, responsibility

URANUS	♅	originality, deviation, urge to reform
NEPTUNE	♆	idealism, inspiration, transcendence
PLUTO	♇	regeneration, death and rebirth

Astrologers also include other factors in the chart: the Moon's Nodes and the asteroid Chiron.

The Moon's Nodes (or the Dragon's Head and the Dragon's Tail) are the two astronomical points where the lunar orbit around the Earth intersects with the Earth's orbit around the Sun. The Lunar Node cycle is 19 years. The South Node (Dragon's Tail) indicates the patterns of the past from which the individual is moving away; the North Node (Dragon's Head) indicates the direction towards which the individual is developing. The North Node is always opposite the South Node, and together they represent an axis which also relates to important contacts or associations in the individual's life.

Chiron is a large asteroid discovered in 1977 between the orbits of Saturn and Uranus. Studies of this body so far suggest that it relates to the archetype of the wounded healer, to teaching and healing work, and to the development of 'heroic' qualities in the face of life's seemingly random injustices.

To understand the meaning of each planet, we observe its physical features, its position in the solar system relative to other bodies, its mythology, and its observed behaviour over time. Each planet will express its own nature according to the zodiac sign it occupies (e.g. Sun in Aries, Moon in Taurus) and its house position in the birth chart (e.g. Sun in the seventh house – relationships, Mars in the tenth house – career). The zodiac signs, the houses and the planetary aspects are explored in Chapters 5, 6 and 7. But first a look at each planetary 'god' in more detail.

THE SUN

If you would create something, you must be something.

GOETHE

The Sun is our nearest star. It is a self-luminous ball of fire which is the source of almost all the solar system's heat, light and energy. From this we may reasonably infer that the Sun is the self-vital principle in any entity. At the biological level, the Sun represents the life-force. At the psychological level, the Sun is the core of individuality, the principle of self-integration that directs and unifies the many different 'selves' within us, the inner guiding light and source of authentic life direction and self-expression. The Sun represents the central focusing point (focus derives from the Greek word for 'fire') of the individual, and hence its association with kingship, authority and creative power.

Just as the Earth orbits around the Sun, the Sun itself is travelling at 1000 miles per second, with the solar system in tow, around the galaxy. The Sun is 'going somewhere' and taking us with it whether we are conscious of it or not. Hence the Sun in the chart symbolizes the inner mind which, when it is focused, will know its own unique life direction.

In Greek mythology the solar principle is Apollo, a name which literally means 'not many'; in other words, unific, one. The Christian Church incorporated pagan Sun-god imagery into the heart of its festivals. Christmas marks the winter solstice, known to the ancient world as the time of the rebirth of the Sovereign Sun, Sol Invictus, the unconquerable spirit, as the days start to grow longer once again. The period around Easter, with its theme of death and resurrection, marks the beginning of the solar year as days become longer than nights.

All heroes and heroines of myth, fairy tale and legend express the essence of the solar ideal. By courageously engaging with the many ordeals of life, we declare our purposes, discover our integrity, and develop confident self-expression. When we are in touch with our solar centre, we *enjoy* life – and we know ourselves to be creative and authentic. When we compromise ourselves too often, we distance ourselves from this centre and end up feeling depressed, devitalized, alien to our real selves. Strongly solar individuals have a commanding presence; they're in the world to be noticed and to be appreciated. They can also be arrogant, vain and tyrannical. If we were to describe the Sun as a character in a novel, he would be the benevolent king, the charismatic leader, the noble and much-respected teacher whose message to all is *carpe diem* – seize the day. The Sun is the main protagonist in our life drama. Solar figures in myth and literature include King Arthur, Hercules and Perseus, to name a few.

The Sun rules the heart, both in the physical and psychological sense. The heart is the central organ of the body, pumping the essential life force – the blood – throughout the entire system. Likewise we feel our essential self is in our heart, the seat of courage, love and generosity. 'I put my *whole heart* into it' is what we say when we dedicate ourselves to something *wholeheartedly*, from the Sun's point of view. The Sun rules fiery Leo, the sign occupied by the Sun in high summer in the northern hemisphere, when its physical heat has reached its maximum. The Sun is exalted in Aries, the first sign of the zodiac, marking the beginning of northern spring, ushered in by Easter, 'the Resurrection', when the days begin to get longer and light triumphs over darkness. By contrast the Sun is said to be in its detriment in Aquarius, the opposite sign to Leo, and in its fall in Libra, the opposite sign to Aries, which brings in the autumn and the beginning of night's victory over day.

The Sun by sign shows the characteristic way in which we centre ourselves as a conscious, purposeful individual – how we 'make up our minds'. In Fire signs, the Sun expresses its will to live with eagerness and enthusiasm. The Sun's essentially intuitive nature and its capacity for inner knowing is emphasized in this element. In Earth signs, the solar purpose is to build and consolidate, to achieve in concrete ways. In Air signs, the Sun manifests its light through thought and communication. In Water signs, the heroic impulse expresses itself through the realm of feeling and profoundly subjective experience. The Sun by house placement shows the specific arena in life which becomes a crucial focus for our personal drama. Aspects to the Sun reveal the gods we encounter – through help or hindrance – on our life's journey. For example, the Sun aspecting Mars (aspect means 'to look at' and in astrology it signifies the dynamic relationship between planets, the way they 'look at' each other) by conjunction makes one a warrior, ready to lead and fight for valued causes; the Sun in a square aspect with Saturn demands that one grapple with authority and responsibility.

THE MOON

I trust that you will grant this boon
O lovely Goddess of the Moon.

OLD CELTIC RITUAL

Swift-moving Luna circles the Earth every month, marking out the ebb and flow of daily life and causing the tidal motions of the seas. Every month we witness her phases as the mysterious crescent Moon changes size and position in the night sky, finally reaching bright fullness and then gradually waning until out of sight completely. The Moon represents this transitional nature of life, the way that one phase organically gives rise to the next, providing us with the experience of connectedness, of being part of some ongoing process. At the most basic psychological level, this ongoing process is our personal past, our family and culture. And more specifically, it is a process that begins with the mother–child bond, that primary relationship where we first experience dependence, containment, and our instinctual needs being met. 'Mother love' is a 'boon' to the infant – his or her survival, and growing sense of identity, depends on it.

The Moon symbolizes the flowing, receptive, feminine aspect of life. The female menstrual cycle is, of course, a lunar one – a month (Moon) long. The Moon represents the impulse to protect and nurture, how we 'mother' and look after ourselves, the daily habit patterns we establish which we take for granted. Solar energy is fiery and immediate whilst lunar energy relates to the body and the binding processes of nature. If we are not grounded in our experience in the specific context of our lives, the Sun cannot achieve its purposes. Hence the equal importance of the Sun and Moon in astrology, and the reason why they are referred to as the two 'lights' or luminaries.

Whilst the Sun relates to our capacity for focused, conscious decision-making, the Moon relates to 'diffuse awareness', to the qualities of our unconscious life and our imagination. The Moon is our most natural and spontaneous response to life, our 'gut level' reactions, how we listen to others and to our own needs, what we need to feel comfortable within ourselves. The Moon is the 'inner' you, the you that has characteristic moods and private feelings which do not ask to be rationally understood but simply accepted and experienced. She is the feminine, feeling atmosphere, the anima of our life drama.

In mythology, Diana the huntress represents one aspect of the Moon. She demands respect for the unconscious, instinctual side of life, and for the sacred procreative power of women.

The goddess Hera signifies another aspect of the Moon, that of the power of matriarchy and the familial bonds which are the basis of all civilization. In fact, the lunar goddess is usually understood in three identities, reflecting the waxing, full, and waning phases of the Moon: the maiden (Persephone), the matron (Hera), and the crone (Hecate).

The Moon by sign shows the characteristic way we feel good about ourselves, the way we nourish ourselves and seek intimacy with others. If your Moon is in a Fire sign, you need passionate play and a safe place to explore your crazy inspirations. If your Moon is in an Earth sign, you need physical affection, order and material security, and good food! If your Moon is in an Air sign, communicating and gaining understanding through the 'digestion of concepts' feels nourishing. If your Moon is in a Water sign, you need deep emotional understanding, non-verbal closeness and sympathy. The Moon by house placement shows the area of life we inhabit instinctively, where we feel 'at home', and where the ebb and flow of life will be keenly felt. Aspects to the Moon significantly qualify the nature of our instinctive responses. If the Moon were a character in a novel, she would be the enigmatic poet, the writer's muse, the devoted mother, the nanny, the therapist and healer, or the professional gourmet cook. A typical Moon type is William Wordsworth (Moon conjunct the Midheaven), the poet who wrote 'I wander lonely as a cloud …'

The Moon rules maternal, full-breasted Cancer, the poetic muse and nourisher who protects and looks after the world as her children. The Moon is exalted in Taurus, the earthy sign of fertility and nature's bounty. The Moon is said to be in its fall in Capricorn, the sign of structure and worldly responsibility. In Scorpio, a sign known for its controlled, brooding intensity, the Moon is in its detriment.

MERCURY

A little learning is a dangerous thing;
Drink deep, or taste not the Pierian spring.

ALEXANDER POPE

Mercury is the swift-moving planet closest to the Sun. In Greek mythology this is Hermes, the Messenger of the Gods, who traverses the boundaries of duality with ease, even being allowed to enter the Underworld with impunity. With wings on his feet, Mercury represents mental activity: language, communication, interpretation, the ability to gather facts and to see relationships between things. It is intellectual curiosity, ingenuity, mobility and adaptability. Although Mercury's province is the nervous system and the activity of mental processes in general, the potential depth of thought will depend on its sign placement and aspects.

Mercury's close proximity to the Sun highlights his role as 'divine conduit' or conductor of solar consciousness, and his psychological function as translator. Its connection with the body is through the five senses, those centres of receptivity that gain knowledge of our world, and through the nervous system that sends messages between the brain and other parts of the body. Mercury makes connections and allows us to put information together, in order to make sense of ourselves in the world. Through Mercury we experience curiosity and apply our minds to learning and communicating. But Mercury is also the trickster and the 'prince of thieves' who lives according to his wit on the boundaries and byways of life. We refer to Mercury as 'he' but this god was always seen as androgynous, easily manifesting through either pole of the masculine–feminine spectrum. Mercury is especially active in the market place and in the arena of politics and theatre, where swiftness and brilliance of intellectual argument can win any debate. Mercury's energy is inventive and clever, but distinctly amoral – ethical concerns belong to other gods. His purpose is to show forth and to bring together the inherent opposites within human nature and life itself.

Mercurial individuals are quick thinkers and fast talkers, often extremely intelligent and learned, and usually wiry and restless with a sensitive nervous system. An excess of Mercurial energy makes one over-cerebral and clever in a trivial way. Mercurial types tend to waste energy through too much thinking and talking. If Mercury were a character in a novel, he would be the inquisitive young student or whiz kid, the suave, bisexual raconteur, the roving reporter, or the crafty, nomadic merchant. A Mercurial figure in literature is Puck in *A Midsummer Night's Dream*, the clever and swift-moving fairy servant of Oberon who, with sleight of hand, makes people seem other than they are. Mercury is the rational principle we employ in our life drama which allows us to learn, to communicate, and sometimes to get by on our wits.

Mercury by sign shows the characteristic way we think and talk. Mercury by house placement reveals specific areas of interest and where we find we express our mental nature best. Aspects to Mercury will qualify our rational energy and the nature of our communicative expression. Mercury rules Gemini and Virgo. In airy Gemini Mercury's innate curiosity, mobility and talkativeness are most evident, whilst in Virgo, an Earth sign, he manifests in a more systematic, practical and diligent manner. In Fire signs Mercury is immediate and visionary but sometimes dogmatic in expression. In Water signs Mercury is imaginative, penetrating and receptive. Mercury is in its fall in moralizing Sagittarius, a sign which likes the big picture and for whom careful analysis does not come easily. Mercury is in its detriment in dreamy, intuitive Pisces, a sign that shuns the tyranny of exact definition. Mercury completes its orbit around the Sun in 88 days.

VENUS

Give beauty all her right!
She's not to one form tied;
Each shape yields fair delight
Where her perfections bide.

THOMAS CAMPION, *BEAUTY UNBOUND*

Venus is the goddess of love and beauty, the Aphrodite of Greek mythology whose grace brought a wondrous, vitalizing energy into the world. Aphrodite's mythical birth can help us understand her energy: she arose in the sea's foam which was created by the severing of her father Uranus's genitals after his conflict with Cronus. This suggests that Venusian energies of diplomacy and appreciation of difference can help to resolve the tensions between warring aims – the old versus the new, the status quo versus change, responsibility versus freedom. This mythic image may also suggest that real beauty is intimately connected with the intense struggles inherent in human life. How do we resolve these struggles? First, we must honour both viewpoints. Venus helps us remain involved in that struggle so we can find out what we really want. Venus represents the need to relate, the desire for love and affection, the urge for co-operation and the appreciation of beauty. Venus is also connected with what we value most, whether this be ideals, relationships, works of art or money.

Venus's rulership of both Taurus and Libra points to her dual nature. Through Taurus we see her lusty side and the showing forth of beauty through physical form. If we remember how hot and steamy it is on Venus, we get a sense of the sexual passions

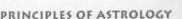

which the great goddess can arouse. Venus displays beauty through colour and form and also through scent and touch. This side of Venus is often seen as the seductress whose romantic appeal can ensnare, but it is true that intense, cathartic relationships always teach us an enormous amount about ourselves. Love and sexuality were always seen in ancient times as bringing a healing reconnection with the vital life force. Through Libra, Venus expresses her beauty in a more idealized and civilized way, through tolerance and the delight in difference. The Libran side of Venus seeks respectful relationships. Here she expresses the urge to enjoy loving connections with others through social encounter, teamwork, fair play, harmony and the reconciliation of opposites.

Venus represents the part of us which easily attracts what we want, rather than going out in 'hot pursuit' (a job for Mars). When we are doing what we love, we radiate vitality and please others – we are popular. Hence, Venus is a 'lucky' energy, bringing us the nice things in life. Strongly Venusian individuals are sociable and friendly, love pleasurable social pursuits and artistic environments, and need others through which to feel balanced and completed. Too much Venus can result in over-indulgence, superficiality, and promiscuity. The function of Venus in the body can be seen in its rulership of the kidneys which cleanse and balance fluid levels. If Venus were a character in a novel, she would be the beautiful romantic heroine – an artist, singer or dancer whose beauty challenges us to passionate, open-hearted encounter; or Venus might also be the kind-hearted, devoted friend who loves and reflects without undue criticism, allowing the other to benefit from truthful, egalitarian friendship. Venus is what we value, attract and enjoy in our life drama.

Venus by sign shows the characteristic way in which we express our affection and our aesthetic and social values. Venus by house placement shows the area in life where we most readily seek enjoyment and express our love of beauty and diplomacy. Aspects to Venus will qualify our need to give and receive affection and our impulse to express beauty. In Fire signs Venus expresses itself through romantic, passionate play and creativity; in Earth signs Venus needs to show affection through demonstrativeness and practical service; in Air signs Venus enjoys lighthearted contact and the delight of verbal interchange; and in Water signs she seeks intimacy and depth with others. Venus is in its fall in self-centred Aries and suspicious Scorpio, and in its detriment in analytical Virgo. Venus completes its orbit of the Sun in 225 days.

MARS

Who is bolder than a lover fighting for his loved one? Mars surpasses the other Gods in fortitude since he makes people strong.

MARSILIO FICINO

Mars is the 'red god', the god of War, the energetic, self-assertive impulse within the human psyche which is necessary for survival. Greek mythology portrays Mars (called Ares) as brutish, short-tempered, impulsive, and always accompanied by his cohorts Deimos (Fear) and Phobos (Fright). The Romans felt the role of Mars was more positive: Honos (Honour) and Virtus (Virtue) always accompanied the Roman Mars. But earlier myths show Mars as a deity connected with vegetation, fertilization and the renewal of nature. This earlier link highlights its instinctive passional and sexual essence. Mars rules Aries and Scorpio, signs connected with spring and autumn when we see transformation taking place in the natural cycle through rebirth and death. The later portrayal of Mars as a god of War contains the qualities of fierce bravery and the courage to face

death – to die for one's cause, one's homeland, and to possess *arete*, the Greek word for honour. In many ancient cultures the spilling of blood pleased the gods and ensured a prosperous harvest. In the natural world, Mars' dynamism expresses itself through the impulse to defend territory and through the sexual drive in animals, ensuring the survival of species. Mars compels the sap to rise in plants. In the human body the Mars principle also expresses itself through the sex drive, the muscles, the red blood cells and adrenaline. This ancient link to natural, elemental power can be seen in images of 'the green man', the wild, tenacious, revitalizing spirit of the forest which was also embodied in the story of Robin Hood. The red planet was always associated with iron and steel. Recent visits to the planet now show that a high proportion of its soil is in fact iron oxide.

The energy of Mars is separative; through this god we say 'no' or 'yes' and then we initiate action. Through Mars we claim our 'rights' and defend our personal worth, much as a cat or dog marks out its own space. When we are thwarted, Mars is our anger – and the way we express that anger. When threatened, adrenaline surges through the body and we suddenly find the energy and courage we need to protect ourselves or to push forward against all odds. This is Mars in action, and like all competitive athletes, he wants to win. But Mars is not just the instinct of self-assertion and competition; we need Mars in order to 'do' anything – Mars is a servant of the Sun, the energy we call upon when we carry out the purposes of the inner hero. Whatever we may decide to do – bake a cake, write a book, learn the game of tennis or pursue a high-powered career – we need Mars to make it happen. A deficiency of Mars produces the 'door mat' personality, someone who cannot defend themselves. When Martial energy is repressed (for example, by strong aspects from Saturn), it can give rise to depression and

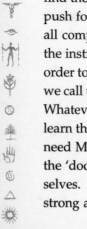

listlessness. If Mars were a character in a novel, he would be the champion athlete or boxer, the brave soldier or trouble-shooter, the confident, risk-taking entrepreneur, or the skilled surgeon who uses a knife to cut out what is not wanted. A typical Mars type is the champion tennis player John McEnroe (Sun square Mars) who also displays an excess of Mars (Mars opposed Jupiter and square Pluto) in his temper. Mars is the energy we use to get what we want and to defend our achievements from attack in the drama of life.

Strongly martial individuals are go-getters, people who love a challenge and are unafraid of vigorous, even dangerous, confrontation. An excess of Mars makes one contentious, quarrelsome, over-aggressive, violent. The martial arts of the East express an important dimension of Mars. They teach the art of self-defence and emphasize the need for disciplining our personal energy. Karate is aggressive, even dangerous and potentially lethal, whilst t'ai chi is gentle and essentially non-aggressive, more to do with the harmonizing of the receptive and projective energies in one's aura.

Mars by sign shows the characteristic way in which we express our self-assertion and drive to succeed. In Fire signs Mars is impulsive and dramatic; in Earth signs Mars is more focused and practical; in Air signs Mars is very observant and expresses through ardent communication; in Water signs he is passionate, moody, and works in fits and starts. Mars by house placements shows the area in life which will be especially 'energized' by our ardent desires and courage to pursue them. Aspects to Mars will qualify this personal energy, and will show how Mars is hindered or enhanced by the other gods. Mars completes its orbit of the Sun in 687 days.

JUPITER

A faith that cannot survive collision with the truth is not worth many regrets.

ARTHUR C. CLARKE

Jupiter is a powerful sky god, the mighty Olympian king we know as Zeus in Greek mythology. Always invoked as the greater *benefic* (an astrological term from the medieval period meaning 'he who bestows benificence'), Jupiter is the god whose blessing one seeks for the success of any enterprise. In mythic tradition he is the great law-giver, supremely masculine and creative, bestowing opportunity, growth and benevolence. Jupiter – or 'Jove' as he is often referred to – gives us the words jovial, joy and jubilation; the very idea of 'en-thusiasm' – *en-theos*, meaning suffused with the energy of the gods – is a Jupiterian one, and indeed Jupiterian individuals are usually bursting with zeal, new ideas and positive feelings. Due to the positive outlook they bring to life, luck is seen to be with them more than any other planetary type.

In mythology, Zeus was forever seeking new lovers, much to the annoyance of his wife and consort Hera, and begetting important children out of wedlock. This part of his story represents the untameable, prolific nature of divine creativity of which humans partake through the prerogative of our intuitive mind. Jupiter is that energy which urges us to expand and to explore beyond the confines of our familiar culture. The Jupiter principle within us also seeks meaning; it urges us to find a rational basis for communal belief – and such beliefs are the very foundations upon which societies are built. Paradoxically, Jupiter is that part of us which bestows faith, the sense that we are connected to all of life in a coherent, intelligent manner, but it also gives us the need to discover truth for ourselves, to arrive at a personal understanding of the larger ideals that bind society together. To discover the enjoyment of intellectual understanding, to conceive of an idea and follow it through to fruition, is a distinctly Jupiterian experience. We feel powerful and godlike! Strongly Jupiterian individuals are the leaders in society; they may also be generous philanthropists or flashy movie stars whose personal dramas are projected out onto the world screen for all to see.

Too much Jupiter makes us 'big-headed' and 'too big for our boots'. In fact, an excess of Jupiter can be very dark indeed: it creates over-indulgence, arrogance, personal inflation and the tendency to 'play god', to feel that we are above the law. Jupiter's excesses may also lead to waste and sloppiness. In the body Jupiter is associated with the liver and the metabolism of fats and sugar, so Jupiter's excesses are quickly evident when they become unhealthy for us. In the negative Jupiter type we can see the tyranny of moral certitude, for the religious or political fanatic often forgets he is part of the mortal human race. Through statistical research, Michel Gauquelin found that Jupiter tended to be prominently placed (angular – that is, near the Ascendant or the Midheaven) in the birth charts of leading Nazis.

If Jupiter were a character in a novel, he would be a powerful governor or president, a wise priest, a lawyer or judge whose knowledge and advice others seek, or a famous, charismatic actor. Mr Toad in *The Wind in the Willows* is an archetypal Jupiterian figure: he is wedded to his enthusiasms, his behaviour is ostentatious, but his warmth and generosity make him loveable and, in slippery circumstances, help him to land on his feet. A typical Jupiter type is the colourful politician and highly successful fiction writer Jeffrey Archer (Sun conjunct Jupiter). Jupiter is the part of us that seeks meaning and benevolent increase in the drama of our life.

Jupiter by sign shows the characteristic way in which we gain and enjoy opportunity and the way we express beliefs and religious faith. Jupiter by house placement shows the area of life which is both blessed by fortune and plagued by over-expectation.

Jupiter rules fiery Sagittarius, the sign of the Archer, who forever propels his arrows onwards and upwards on a journey of discovery. Jupiter is the co-ruler of Pisces, another sign connected with religion and compassion. In Fire signs Jupiter is speculative, enterprising, independent; in Earth signs Jupiter expands ambitions for material security and status; in Air signs Jupiter is philosophical, sociable, and enthusiastic about ideas; in Water signs Jupiter is intuitive, magnetic and charitable. Jupiter completes its orbit of the Sun in 12 years.

SATURN

Saturn is not simply a troublesome planet to be avoided; with perseverance and endurance we may find in his dark, heavy, ambivalent moods a way through and beyond the shallowness of the present.

THOMAS MOORE

Saturn is Chronos, Father Time, chronology, the ancient ruler of fate, limits, responsibilities and structure. Traditionally depicted with a scythe and known as the Grim Reaper and the Lord of Karma, Saturn has always inspired dread and fear, for this is the god who brings obstacles and trials and who is related to pain, loneliness and endings. But by surviving and finally learning through such trials, we become stronger and chisel out a real identity. Without Saturn, Jupiter's propensity to expand would soon render our experience meaningless; and, in fact, Jupiter's urge to grow immediately invokes Saturn's function, which is to define and to give finite structure, to make things manifest and tangible. Saturn's purpose within the human psyche is to give endurance, determination and discipline so that our purposes can be achieved.

Saturn evokes in us the fear that we won't be up to the demands of life, that when put to the test, we will be found wanting. Saturn's position in the horoscope indicates the way we are likely to handle anxiety. But, more positively, it shows where our centre of gravity is, and where we are most inclined to 'put our weight' behind things and 'earth' our vision. Our hopes and wishes do not manifest themselves magically, but rather they require of us hard work – blood, sweat, and tears – and a patient, systematic approach. Saturn's work can be alchemical, in that with time and hard work we turn the base metal of ourselves into gold.

In mythology Saturn is a jealous god who devours his children in order to maintain his rule and authority. Through the trickery of his wife Rhea, Saturn is overthrown by his son Zeus and is then relegated to the background, to the kingdom of the Golden Age. This story reveals the quality of the senex, the old man who stands for the past, the status quo, and the old order. The negative qualities of the senex are arrogance, pride and cruel retaliation against anything fresh and innovative. But the principles we rebel against remain firmly rooted in our psyches and therefore within our essential identity. This is a positive contribution of Saturn the senex.

Saturnine individuals are serious, conservative and self-controlled; they may suffer depression and repress emotional need. But these individuals can also be very self-reliant, dependable, resourceful and wise, and their integrity offers a sense of stability and comfort to others. Just as Saturn can be supportive to others, its role in the body is to structure and support through the skeletal system, as well as giving boundaries

and definition through the skin and connective tissue. Saturnine individuals usually feel a strong need to make a useful and recognizable contribution to society. If Saturn were a character in a novel, he would be a sublimely rational scientist, a judge, a builder or farmer, or an ancient hermit living on a mountaintop. A typical Saturn type is the Conservative Prime Minister Margaret Thatcher (Saturn exactly rising) who emphasized the need for every individual to assume personal responsibility.

Saturn by sign shows the characteristic way in which we experience authority, obstacles and fear in life, as well as the kind of tasks which help us develop discipline and maintain commitment in order to realize our goals. Saturn by house placement shows the area of life where we have to work the hardest, sometimes over-compensating for a sense of inadequacy but other times successfully journeying through phases which reward us with a more substantial sense of self. When Saturn aspects another planet, that energy will be restricted, disciplined, turned inward.

Saturn is the ruler of ambitious, earthy, aspiring Capricorn. Saturn also co-rules Aquarius, a detached air sign dedicated to impartial analysis in the service of truth. Saturn is said to be in its fall in Cancer, a sign of fluidity and emotional need, and also in Leo, a sign devoted to enjoyment of the self and its creations. It is in its exaltation in Libra, a sign that loves the justice and beauty of exact, intellectual principles. In Aries, a sign whose impetuous energy resents the stability of Saturn, this planet is said to be in its detriment. In Fire signs, Saturn strives to develop self-confidence and faith in his visions. In Earth signs, Saturn is dogged and purposeful, aiming for solid, material accomplishment. In Air signs, Saturn seeks security through objective experience and rational certainty. In Water signs, Saturn strives to transform emotional fears into depth of understanding. Saturn completes its orbit of the Sun in 29 years.

URANUS

> The heavenly vision of Uranus may sometimes seem impersonal and cold, yet it offers us greater freedom through a new and broader perspective on our lives.
>
> LIZ GREENE

The discovery of Uranus by William Herschel in Bath in 1781 completely upset the neat planetary symbolism of the past many thousands of years. Until that time Saturn was understood to be 'the ring pass not', the outermost boundary of the world prior to the Fixed Stars. The meaning of Uranus is congruent with this idea of breaking through boundaries and the disarrangement of fixed structures. Uranus was discovered as the world was entering its most radical phase, with revolutions erupting in Europe and the newly colonized America. A spirit of rebellion was born, aimed against the fated sense of class distinctions and oppression. The demands of Uranus could be heard in the familiar slogan of the French Revolution – *'liberté, egalité, fraternité'*. Uranus is the energy within the human psyche which rejects the limits of the status quo in the service of individuality and independence, and it sees these as inalienable rights of every individual.

There are two myths which tell us something about this energy. Ouranos was the great sky god whose marriage to Gaea, ruler of the Earth, produced the Titans. Ouranos rejected his offspring as ugly and imperfect. He was later overthrown by his son Chronos, who was subsequently ousted by his own son Zeus. We see in this how the impulse to rebel creates its own rhythm: the new order eventually becomes the status quo which must be confronted and overthrown. The other myth is that of Prometheus who defied Zeus in stealing divine fire from Mount Olympus to give to man who was stumbling in the

darkness of earthly life. This fire is the creative power of 'nous' or mind, which freed man from complete bondage to his animality; this was the beginning of true human culture. Prometheus's act of challenging divine law was an enormous risk, and he was cruelly punished by Zeus afterwards. Uranians are risk-takers: with insight that sees beyond normal boundaries, and with courage to shock society with radically different views, they are the visionaries who take society towards a brave new world. But they often pay dearly for their boldness.

Uranus is that energy within us that seeks new breakthroughs, new freedom, new understanding. But whether or not we integrate Uranian energies wisely depends upon how well we have learned the lessons of Saturn, whose practicality and realism help us avoid a continuing round of anarchic chaos. Aspects between these two gods are important in telling us how these two energies will negotiate their respective needs within us.

Strongly Uranian individuals are often seen as eccentric outsiders who bring a message society needs to hear. They often defend the underdog, and remind society that everybody has a 'mad' – or acutely original – bit which needs acceptance. If Uranus were a character in a novel, he would be the social reformer, the mathematical or astronomical genius, or the outspoken playwright whose insights irrevocably change our view of the world. A typical Uranus type is Sigmund Freud (Sun conjunct Uranus) whose genius opened up the whole new frontier of man's inner mind. Another Uranian is the highly eccentric comedian Spike Milligan (Uranus exactly rising in Aquarius). Uranus is associated with the nervous system in the body, and in the natural world with lightning and earthquakes.

Uranus by sign shows the characteristic way in which we deviate from the norm and attempt to express our originality. Uranus by house placement shows the area of life which will see many changes and sudden new perceptions. When Uranus aspects another planet, that energy will be challenged (creating an inner tension) or 'electrified', in some way speeded up, by Uranus's independent spirit. In Fire signs, Uranus is indomitable and awakens the pioneering urge. In Earth signs, Uranus is obstinate and awakens constructive resourcefulness. In Air signs, Uranus is ingenious, persuasive and awakens mental energies. In Water signs, Uranus is intuitive and intense, and awakens the imagination.

Uranus rules Aquarius, a sign whose viewpoint is often challenging and prophetic. Its fall is in Leo, a sign which values individual nobility and kingliness. Uranus completes its orbit of the Sun in 84 years.

NEPTUNE

Although we often speak of 'finding ourselves,' that is, of discovering our unique identity or defining ourselves through self-chosen attributes and achievements, Neptune is the opposite: it is the urge to lose ourselves, to dissolve or transcend the boundaries of the isolated ego.

HOWARD SASPORTAS

Neptune is the God of the sea who rules the watery depths both of nature and of man's emotional imagination. The discovery of this planet in 1846 punctuated a period in which many Neptunian developments occurred: the consolidation of steam power for travel, the use of anaesthetics for pain relief, the rise of spiritualism, and the increase of a social conscience which brought homes for the poor. Neptune represents the oneness of all life from which springs the sense of an invisible, mystical bond between ourselves and others – and this is the source of compassion, our capacity to feel in and with another.

Water is a substance in which things dissolve and which seeks to erode boundaries. This is a Neptunian quality, and within the human psyche it is that urge to merge, to experience blissful union with another. In human experience we can see this primarily as the intrauterine condition of the foetus, whose existence is an unawakened symbiosis with the mother. Falling in love is a kind of Neptunian romantic 'spell' where we long to belong utterly to the beloved. Likewise, the goal of all religions is essentially a Neptunian one: union with the Divine. Pantheistic religions exalt that state of oneness with nature. Anathema to all these ideas of oneness is that of struggling separately in an objective world of piercing definition, where we have to develop self-reliance and earn our sense of self-worth.

Neptune's province is the unseen world of fantasy and myth, dreams and visions, that realm of magic and beauty that transcends everyday limits. It brings the capacity for inspired artistic creativity and is strong in the charts of artists, actors and musicians, as well as highly gifted healers and therapists. But it is a tricky energy to use in ordinary life, as Neptune's longings for perfect love and the elimination of pain often remain operative in an unconscious way, adopting circuitous escape routes to avoid the harsh lessons of the school of life. For this reason, it can make us gullible, prone to delusions, and less able to discern what is objectively real. This pertains especially to people with very weak ego structures and who take escape routes through drugs and alcohol. Saturnine realism and discipline is an invaluable antidote to Neptunian vulnerability.

Neptunian energy projects a fragile yet beguilingly charismatic appeal. Sometimes the whole gamut of its expressions may be observed: grandiosity and selflessness, glamour and unworldliness, sensuality and saintliness, artistic inspiration and a sense of unworthiness. Neptune can ensnare us in a victim–saviour dynamic, or it can uplift us through consciousness-

expanding experiences. In the body Neptune rules the lymphatic system which recognizes and destroys foreign entities. If Neptune were a character in a novel, he would be the inspired musician or artist, the saint or mystic, the seductively glamorous movie star, or the down-and-out alcoholic. A typical Neptune type is the inspired composer Mozart (Sun opposed Neptune). Another example is Jung (Sun square Neptune), the psychologist who explored the archetypal depths of the unconscious through experiencing his own psychotic breakdown.

Neptune rules watery, enigmatic and versatile Pisces. Its fall is in Virgo, a sign which strives for analytical precision. Neptune by sign shows the characteristic way we express our imagination, compassion, and desire for romantic and spiritual unity. Neptune by house placement shows the area of life we are prone to romanticize and where we may have to experience sacrifice. When Neptune aspects another planet, that energy is especially sensitized, maybe weakened, but always endowed with a dreamy, imaginative quality. In Fire signs Neptune holds a passionate optimism and idealizes the drama and nobility of the human spirit. In Earth signs Neptune holds a romantic vision of practical service and material wellbeing. In Air signs Neptune idealizes relationships and holds a utopian view of social harmony and the power of reason to redeem mankind. In Water signs Neptune idealizes intimacy and yearns for a deep sense of belonging. Neptune completes its orbit of the Sun in 165 years.

PLUTO

The nature of Pluto is similar to that of the Hindu god Shiva, the creator and destroyer: it begins by breaking down a structure, then it creates a new one in its place.

ROBERT HAND

Pluto is the powerful elemental force which impels the growth and evolution of all life forms. It represents the unseen forces that work away below the surface and which periodically erupt into conscious awareness. This last planet in our solar system was discovered in 1930, a time which ushered in the use of atomic power. Of course, plutonium is the active ingredient in the atomic bomb. This discovery marked a pivotal point of no return in mankind's history: will we use this power creatively or destructively? This was also the period that saw the rise of fascism, of large-scale gangster networks, as well as a more widespread acceptance of depth psychoanalysis.

Pluto is Hades, god of the Underworld, who kidnapped the young and innocent Persephone to be his wife and consort in the realm of the dead. Demeter's agony at the loss of her daughter created a horrible drought and nothing would grow. Zeus therefore ruled that Persephone was allowed to return to the world for two-thirds of the year, but her marriage to Hades was irreversible. Her descent and transformation are the crux of Pluto's energy: it rules the fundamental transformational processes of life – birth, sex and death. At the deepest level, Pluto is the mystery of death and rebirth.

Pluto's realm is that of intense upheaval and transformation and the cathartic release of energy we can observe in natural disasters, the birth process, or a psychological breakdown or breakthrough. Pluto's energy is Freud's id and the biological and psychological drives which push us relentlessly towards transformation. Change can bring fear, and Plutonian individuals tend to be control freaks, obsessive in their need to dominate or restrain others. Underneath this resistance is fear of the overwhelming force of their own primitive urges. Societies also resist, or attempt to contain, Plutonian urges through the phenomena of taboos: certain behaviours are outlawed (e.g. incest, polygamy). Plutonian power can be abused, and those with a prominent Pluto know this instinctively. They therefore can be suspicious and secretive, expecting the worst from others through experience, or through being tuned into their own darkest thoughts. Plutonian individuals who have suffered damaging abuse need to find a way to use their experience, for they can become powerful agents of healing for others.

Plutonians are often attracted to mysteries and want to get to the bottom of things; hence, they are often found in police work, scientific and medical research, paranormal studies and psychoanalytical work where an essential quality is the courage to face pain and difficult truths. Whilst coming through these underworld journeys can be painful, we can emerge with a sense of having retrieved a bit of buried treasure. If Pluto were a character in a novel, he would be a secret agent, a magician or alchemist, a wealthy tycoon living behind the protection of private guards, or a powerful political leader. Two very different Pluto types are Elisabeth Kubler-Ross (Sun conjunct Pluto), the therapist for the terminally ill and author of *On Death and Dying*, and the revolutionary Chinese leader, Mao Tse Tung (Sun/Moon = Pluto).

Pluto by sign shows the characteristic way that we experience the force of our basic urges, and are impelled towards transformations. Pluto by house placement shows the area of life that will be empowered and changed through Plutonian intensity and regeneration. When Pluto aspects another planet, that energy will be greatly intensified and will be a source of major personal transformation. Pluto rules Scorpio, the sign of passionate desire and penetrating insight. It is in its fall in Taurus, a stolid, imperturbable Earth sign that resists change. In Fire signs Pluto's power comes through an intense desire to be creative, and to affect others through personal expression. In Earth signs Pluto's power comes through an intense desire for material order, efficiency, security and permanence. In Air signs Pluto's power comes through communication and an intense belief in the regenerative influence of ideas. In Water signs Pluto's power comes through an intense desire for intimacy, emotional maturity, and the healing power of love. Pluto completes its orbit of the Sun in 248 years.

CHIRON

Your pain is the breaking of the shell
that encloses your understanding.

KAHIL GIBRAN

Discovered in 1977, Chiron is an asteroid or comet which was caught in the solar system's gravitational pull between the orbits of Saturn and Uranus. After 20 years of observation and research, it has been recognized as a very important dimension of the birth chart. In Greek mythology Chiron was the greatest of the Centaurs, that race of half-horse and half-human beings which represent the primitive force of the instincts being guided by conscious intelligence. Chiron was a great teacher and healer who suffered the misfortune of being accidentally struck by an arrow of Hercules. The arrow was tainted with the blood of the Hydra so inflicted Chiron with an agonizing and incurable wound. Due to his immortality, he could not escape his pain through death, and so he turned his suffering into the wisdom and healing powers which benefited many.

Transformed by his wound, Chiron became a civilizing force for his own race and directed them into more orderly, respectful habits which allowed them to enjoy comradeship with human beings.

Chiron represents the wound which life's inherent unfairness brings to everyone. That unfairness is often due to historical and social realities, such as war and natural disasters, and therefore it is difficult finding anyone to blame. The great Centaur's response to his never-ending pain was to accept it, learn from it, and offer others the benefit of his excruciating experience, for after enduring such pain he could understand others' suffering and teach with profound compassion. Chiron represents the wound which spurs us on to grapple with seemingly pointless suffering. Chironic wounds can make us bitter and cynical about life, for suddenly the universe appears to be anything but benign. But by 'staying with' the pain, and sharing the struggle with others, we can find resources within that help us to make sense of the most inexplicable experiences. This is Chiron's heroism – making a choice that brings out inherent nobility. By choosing to respond with integrity and wisdom, we can become a source of healing for others. Chiron's orbit around the Sun is approximately 50 years.

DIVINE DIALOGUES – THE ASPECTS

Language is the light of the mind.

JOHN STUART MILL

THE CIRCULAR STAGE

On the circular stage of the birth chart (Figure 5.1) are depicted and enacted the essential features of a life's drama: its specific talents, challenges, joys, confusions, tensions, inconsistencies, friendships, crises and resolutions. The planets are the actors. Each actor's script is determined by its position on each of three different circles around the stage:

- The planet's **sign** position *(see Chapter 6)* – its position in the cycle of the zodiac, which tells us its characteristic mode of expression.

- The planet's **house** position *(see Chapter 7)* – its position in the daily cycle, which tells us in which area of life its activities are most likely to be expressed and experienced.

- The planet's position along its circle of relationship with each of the other planets. This shows the **aspects** or **harmonics** the planet is making with the other planets.

These reveal who is talking to whom, and the likely nature of the relationship and their dialogue.

This chapter focuses on the aspects between the planets, a term which comes from the Latin verb *aspicere* – 'to look at'.

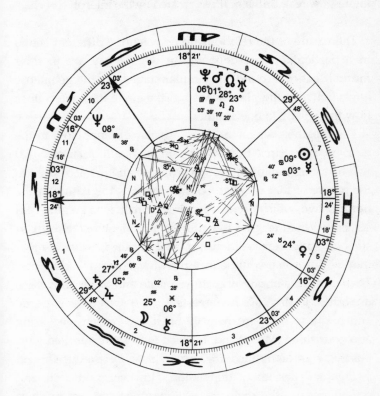

Figure 5.1. The Chart can be seen as a circular stage on which the planets act out their dramas. The twelve signs of the zodiac around the outside are the backdrops for the action. The twelve houses marked in the circle inside the zone demarcate the different areas of life in which the planets act out their stories. The lines in the central circle, show the kind of relationship between the planets, the aspects.

WHO IS TALKING TO WHOM?

In the last chapter we considered the nature of the planetary gods, their different functions, energies and needs. But whilst planets can, and do, at times speak in soliloquies and monologues, the real drama of life is created by the interplay of characters.

The nature of the relationship between the different actors in a particular chart depends on where they are in their mutual 'dance' around the circular stage. It is the geometric angle between the planets around the circle that determines how they relate to one another.

Those planets which are at an angular distance close to the division of the circle by a whole number *(see Table on page 102)* will be brought into connection with one another according to the nature of that number. So, for example, the nature of the number two, which divides the circle in half, is to polarize and objectify. When we find two planets, say Moon and Saturn, in such an opposition relationship, as it is called, we know that they will in some way be in a tug-of-war within the psyche. There will be a strong need to reconcile and work with these opposites. In this case it suggests a tug between the capacity and desire to be spontaneously open and responsive, caring and nourishing (Moon) and the need to be self-controlled, purposeful and disciplined (Saturn). This may produce mood swings and periods of depression. However, with time and self-awareness, the dialogue in this opposition can produce someone who is in some way a professional (Saturn) mother (Moon), perhaps a nurse, carer, restaurateur, nutritionist or gardener. As we shall see in Figure 5.2 (phases), each pair of planets goes through a complete cycle of relationships as their relative motions bring them together and then apart again in an endless dance.

To understand what an aspect is, we need to remind ourselves that, over time, each planet moves through a cycle of 360° with each other planet. We are all familiar with this cycle from the monthly phases of the Moon. The Moon is in 'conjunction', i.e. together in the sky with, the Sun at New Moon. Because the Moon moves much faster, it gradually moves ahead of the Sun, until about seven days later it is 90° from the Sun, the First Quarter, known as the outgoing 'square' aspect. Then seven days later again it reaches Full Moon when it is 180° or in 'opposition' aspect to the Sun in the sky. At that point it begins to move back towards the Sun. Some seven days later it forms the Last Quarter or incoming 'square' aspect and then finally, after a total of about 28 days, it conjoins the Sun again to form the next New Moon.

The total cycle is seen as symbolic of the natural process of growth and decay, analogous to the seasons of the year. At the New Moon, the conjunction, the seed is planted. It works in the earth and springs through the soil at the First Quarter. It develops, blossoms, is fertilized and a new seed is set at the Full phase. The developing fruit ripens and falls at the Last Quarter and gradually decays back into the ground to prepare for the new cycle of growth which begins again at the conjunction.

Whilst these phases mark four of the most important aspects in the cycle, the ever-changing relationship is in fact a continuous process. Each phase has its significance and contributes to the total unfoldment. And in practice the astrologer identifies several other distinct phases in the dance.

THE ASPECT GRID

Planets can be seen together in the sky and then gradually separating as they move through a 360° relationship with one another. At each phase of this cycle their relationship will be different. For example, if two planets are close together, 'in conjunction', they will, for better or worse, be obliged to talk and work with one another. On the other hand, if they stand on opposite sides of the circle they will be 'in opposition' and tend to oppose and contradict one another.

To discover which planets are on talking terms, the astrologer calculates, or has the computer produce, an aspect grid (see Figure 5.2) and will usually show these connections between the planets with lines of different colours. The aspect grid and the lines show which planets are 'in aspect' or 'in a harmonic relationship', i.e. separated by distances which are close to a whole number division of the circle. The colour of the line will indicate the quality of the relationship. Harmonious aspects (see 'Co-operating or Quarrelling', page 108) are usually marked in blue, whereas tense, challenging relationships are marked in red, but this will depend on the colour associations of the individual astrologer.

All of the aspects in a chart will have some significance, but it is especially important to establish the relationships of the main characters, such as the Sun and Moon, the hero and heroine, as it were, of any chart, and the ruling planet. If a planet is entirely unaspected, it is a loner and may create its own dramas.

NUMBER: ESTABLISHING THE QUALITY OF THE DIALOGUE

Aspects are based on the distance planets are apart around the circular stage. The degrees of separation – the angular distance – between any two planets will be a particular fraction or harmonic of the circle. For example, the opposition is half a circle, it is ½, one divided by two or the second harmonic. The quality of the relationship between the planets will be determined by the nature of the number by which the circle is divided. So when two planets are 180° apart, in opposition, in a second harmonic relationship, their association will take on the characteristics of Two-ness, i.e. it will be concerned with objective expression, with polarization and the potential for manifestation. When 120° apart, planets will resonate to the idea of Three-ness, which brings out a sense of beauty and harmony in the relationship and will find expression in an ease and delight in working together. And so on with each number.

Hence, to really understand the significance of the aspects, and indeed the signs and houses, we need to learn the basics of numerology. This is a profound study in itself and can only be touched upon here. Some brief indications are given in the paragraphs on each of the main aspects.

The Table on page 102 gives a summary of each of the first 12 aspects. The 11th harmonic aspect is included for completeness, although it and its multiples are not currently in common use. In theory the division of the circle by any number will have its own particular meaning, adding subtler shades of meaning to the final picture.

ORBS

In any particular chart, planets are seldom found to be exactly aspecting one another. The 'orb' given in the final column of the following table indicates the distance, in degrees, from the exact aspect at which that kind of relationship between the planets will begin to be felt. As in everyday life, planets do not have to be exactly alongside one another in order to enter into a dialogue. When planets get 'within orb' they can, as it were, hear each other. The closer planets get to an exact aspect, the more intense and clear cut their conversation. As they separate from each other, they gradually move out of earshot, and will lose connection until they come into orbs of another aspect. The orbs listed are rough indications based on observation and experience over many years. In any particular chart, orbs may be extended if the planets involved are prominent or form part of a larger aspect pattern.

The Aspects or Harmonics

Aspect	Division of 360 by	Angle	Symbol	Orb
CONJUNCTION	1	0	☌	8
OPPOSITION	2	180	☍	8
TRINE	3	120	△	5
SQUARE	4	90	□	5
QUINTILE	5	72	Q	4
BI-QUINTILE	2/5	144	BQ	4
SEXTILE	6	60	✳	4
SEPTILE	7	51° 26	1/7 S	2° 30
BI-SEPTILE	2/7	102° 51	2/7 BS	2° 30
TRI-SEPTILE	3/7	154° 18	3/7 TS	2° 30
SEMI-SQUARE	8	45	△	2

SESQUIQUADRATE	3/8	135	⊡	2
NOVILE	9	40	1/9 or N	1° 40
DECILE	10	36	1/10 or D	1° 30
ELEVENTH	11	32° 44*	1/11	1
SEMI-SEXTILE	12	30	⊻	1
QUINCUNX	5/12	150	⊼	2

* The Eleventh harmonic is not in common use.

The orbs given are based on experience. Somewhat wider orbs can be used when the Sun and Moon are involved. Aspects are most powerful when closest to exactitude.

THE OUTGOING AND INCOMING PHASES

Figure 5.2 illustrates the cycle of aspects using the monthly dance between Moon and Sun. This is the basic model for all pairs of planets. We can see that, in fact, the Moon goes through the above sequence of aspects twice in its monthly cycle with the Sun. The first time, following the New Moon, when she is moving away from the Sun, is known as the outgoing or waxing phase. The second time, as the Moon continues her journey back towards the Sun, is called the incoming or waning phase.

Thus there are two forms of each aspect. For example, we see the outgoing or waxing square, the First Quarter, when, following the New Moon, the Moon has moved on 90° from the Sun. Then, following the Full Moon, there is the incoming or waning square, the Last Quarter, when the Moon has 90° left of its journey to the next New Moon.

It will be seen that, whilst these two aspects appear to be identical, the waxing square relates to a time when there is the

	☽	☉	☿	♀	♂	♃	♄	♅	♆	♇	⚷	☊	As	Mc
☽					# 0A59				// 0A14				# 0A47	
☉	⚼ 0S22													# 0A09
☿		☌ 6S27			# 0S50									
♀	□ 0S38	∠ 0A15	N 1S11											
♂	☍ 6A36	S 0A33	✶ 1A33						# 0A45				// 0S11	
♃		S^3 0S16	⚼ 1S53	D^3 1S18	S^3 0S50									
♄			S^3 1A06	△ 3A24	Q^2 2A10	☌ 7A16				# 0A17				
♅	☍ 1S42	∠ 1S19	S 1A17	□ 1S03		S^3 0A11								
♆	D^3 1A35	△ 1S01	△ 5S26			□ 3S32	^{2} 0S49						# 0A33	
♇		✶ 3S37	✶ 2S50	S^2 1S12	☌ 4A23	⚼ 0S56	Q^2 2S13		✶ 2A35					
⚷		△ 3S11	△ 3S15		☌ 4A49	N 1S22	N 1A20		△ 2S10	☌ 0A25				
☊	☍ 3A07				□ 3A46	☌ 3S28		⚼ 0S21	☌ 4A50	Q 1S32	☌ 7S52			
As		N^4 1S15		S^3 1S42	D^3 1S14	∠ 1A41	N 0S35	△ 4S55	N 0A13	S^2 0S29				
Mc	△ 1S59	S^2 0A32			⚼ 1S20	S 0S01	S^2 0S48	□ 4A45	✶ 0S16			∠ 2A00	⚼ 1S35	

Figure 5.2. The Aspect grid shows the angular relationship, the aspect, between each pair of planets. The main aspects are shown in the lower left triangular grid. The top right grid shows those planets whose orbits are in parallel or contra-parallel, i.e. at the same angles north or south of the equator.

challenging pressure produced by an impatient spring-like desire to build up and move out into the world and get to grips with the principles involved. By contrast, the incoming square relates to the challenge of the autumnal process of harvesting and giving back the ideas of the cycle to the world. For example, Jung was born with the outgoing square of Sun to Neptune. His life was spent getting to grips with individuating (Sun) himself and his patients from the Collective (Neptune). By contrast, the medical missionary Albert Schweitzer, who had the incoming square, spent his life honing his creative gifts (Sun) in music, theology, philosophy and medicine so that he could better give his life (Sun) back in sacrifice to the lepers and sick (Neptune) of Lamberene.

THE RELATIVE STRENGTH OF ASPECTS

The closest aspects in a chart will always be of importance, and the qualities of the planets involved are likely to be strong in the character. However, aspects are not of equal importance. As a rule, we can say that the closer the divisor of the circle is to unity (number one), the more universal will be the significance of the aspect; the more remote the number from unity, the more particular will be the aspect's qualities and meaning.

So, for example, the conjunction, which is based on the number one or unity, is by far the most important aspect. By contrast, an aspect based on, say, the division of the circle by 17, will have a very particular meaning, which would only be of significance to a highly experienced expert fine-tuning a chart reading.

THE COSMIC DANCE UNFOLDS THE PLANETARY IDEAS

The planets are constantly circling the Sun and changing their relationships with one another. These changing positions in the dance come about because the planets move at very different speeds. As we saw in the last chapter, Mercury, which is the closest planet to the Sun, takes just 88 days to complete one orbit, whilst Pluto, the most distant, takes some 246 years.

Because of this difference in speed, a faster planet can be seen to catch up with a slower planet, join it for a moment, the moment of 'conjunction', and then move on ahead, as shown in Figure 5.2. In due course, the faster planet arrives at a point in its orbit at which it is opposite the slower planet, the 'opposition'. It then moves on round to the next conjunction. This cycle from conjunction to conjunction is the basic element in the cosmic dance. The aspects mark out the different main stages of this cycle.

It is these cycles that, as Plato's 'instruments of time', are constantly unfolding the formative eternal ideas of the planets into our individual and collective consciousness. The birth chart, as a freeze-frame picture of one moment in this ever-changing dance, depicts the particular combination of creative ideas that are being released at that moment.

GOING RETROGRADE

Viewing the dance of the heavens from Earth further complicates the picture. For whilst the planets are steadily circling the Sun in one direction, there will be times when, viewed from Earth, a planet will appear to slow down, stop and move backwards with increasing speed across the sky, to 'go retrograde' (see Figure 5.3). Then, after a while, the planet will slow down, apparently stop and then move forward again with increasing speed. This means that the relationship between any two planets during their mutual cycle goes through a kind of 'pause' and 'emphasis' phase. These retrograde periods highlight important times when unfinished business relating to the two principles can be more thoroughly grappled with, and sometimes resolved. For example, when Mercury is retrograde it suggests that the mind is more inwardly directed and that instead of simply communicating outwardly there is a greater

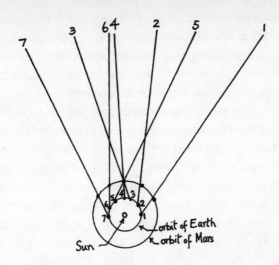

Figure 5.3. Retrograde motion (shown by the symbol R) is the apparent 'moving backwards' of a planet in relation to the Earth. In its orbit
around the Sun, the Earth overtakes it atr the point of opposition. At
position one, two, and three, the planet moves forward; at four and
five, it is seen to move backwards; at six and seven it moves forward
again. In the bith chart, retrograde planets seem to have a more
intense and introverted influence.

capacity for reflective thought. If Mercury is retrograde in
aspect to Saturn it shows a very strong critical sense and desire
to engage with, understand and unravel problems.

UNFOLDING IDEAS

In Platonic terms, each cycle, from conjunction to conjunction,
unfolds a basic idea or theme. So the cycle of Mercury-Pluto
unfolds the changing relationship between individual mind
(Mercury) and the deep urge to survive and have the power to
control and shape the world (Pluto). When on good terms (i.e.

in harmonious aspect), these two can produce penetrating thought, acute intellectual analysis, and great powers of persuasion. When arguing with one another (i.e. in a tense aspect), there is a preoccupation with survival issues, suspicion, verbal power struggles, and a tendency to paranoia.

You may be a strongly mercurial type. But what do you talk about? And how do other facets of your personality get on with your endless curiosity and nervous energy? A study of the geometrical relationship of Mercury to the other planets in the chart will help answer such questions.

If your Mercury and Mars are on talking terms, i.e. in aspect with one another, we need to know whether their conversation is generally convivial, tense and argumentative, high-flown, practically constructive, intellectually stimulating, or even inspiring.

CO-OPERATING OR QUARRELLING?

Trines and sextiles are traditionally considered to be soft, easy, harmonious, good or 'benefic' aspects. Oppositions, squares, semi-squares and sesquiquadrates are considered to be difficult, hard, inharmonious, 'malefic' or evil aspects. There is some truth in this in as far as the easy aspects between planets do produce co-operation and mutual encouragement, whilst the hard aspects usually indicate some measure of tension and produce the challenge to 'get to grips' with the issues involved and make things happen. In practice, however, aspects can indicate much subtler shades of meaning, and hard aspects often 'deliver the goods' whilst soft aspects may generate great aspirations but little of the necessary perspiration to make things happen.

Aspects, like relationships, come in many varieties. Some are simple and straightforward; others are subtler and more complex. Thus the conjunction, when two planets are standing next to one another, demands that these two gods will have to get used to living together, or 'in each other's pockets': a close relationship is inevitable. Whether or not it is a happy coexistence will depend on:

- the essential nature of the partners;

- the sign they are placed in – *(see Chapter 6)*;

- the house they are standing in – *(see Chapter 7)*.

For example, Venus and Jupiter both like the good things in life, and each will easily fan the other's happy expectations. But Venus and Saturn in conjunction is more of a marriage of opposites and makes for harder work. Venus relates through her feelings. She is delighted by the beautiful in all its forms. She desires to experience happiness through a love which merges herself and her lover in total oneness. Saturn, by contrast, is an essentially intellectual god. He seeks order and needs to establish and clarify boundaries, to be cautious, factual and reserved. However, if Venus and Saturn are in the sign Libra, this could be very much more harmonious, as both planets 'joy' (the technical term used to mean very happy) in this sign, which brings out the intellectual and justice-seeking qualities of both planets. If, on the other hand, Venus and Jupiter meet in Virgo, a sign in which both feel relatively uncomfortable, their dialogue is likely to be far more restrained, cautious and abstemious than one would normally expect of these two party-goers.

So, too, the house in which a planet is standing will be more or less congenial and will have its impact on the quality of the

relationship and the focus of the conversation. Venus and Saturn in the second house are more likely to be interested in discussing values and economic matters, whilst in the fifth, their preoccupations will be more obviously creative and concerned with personal self-expression.

THE CYCLE OF ASPECTS

There is no room in this short book to give even a brief account of each of the planetary combinations. Instead, here are some essential factors about each of the aspects. Examples of the Sun and Neptune at each phase are used to illustrate the principles involved.

THE CONJUNCTION – THE NUMBER ONE

$360/1 = 360$. The first harmonic. Life starts with the union of opposites, with the coming together of male and female. The conjunction represents the beginning of a cycle and suggests a merging of principles. When male and female are conjoined, as in marriage, they are brought together in unity. But marriage is not just a union. Just as a fertilized seed contains subjectively within itself all the vast potential that can spring forth from that pregnant unity, so the conjunction aspect is fully of potency. Lord Mountbatten, Admiral of the Fleet during the Second World War, was born with $\odot\sigma\Psi$.

THE OPPOSITION

As we have seen, this is the number of polarity. In terms of the divine descent from unity into multiplicity, two represents the primary moment of ex-pression.

The opposition (180°) occurs when planets are placed on opposite sides of the circle, suggesting confrontation, tension and, eventually, complementariness. Again, the degree of tension generated from this aspect is determined by the nature of the planets involved. If the Sun is in opposition to Neptune, for example, there will be a constant tug between the desire for purposeful, individual self-expression (Sun) and a tendency to abandon oneself to float on the great sea of life and the collective unconscious (Neptune). The individual (Sun) will either be fed by the collective and become immensely creative, insightful and imaginative, or fall in and drown.

Mozart is a classic ☉☌♆, both highly individual and yet plugged into the collective so that inspiration poured through him. 'I write as a cow pees,' he was reported to have said. The ☉☌♆ is reflected at another level in his deeply ambiguous relationship with his father (Sun).

THE TRINE

If the opposition puts the opposing view, the antithesis, then the trine, which brings in a third view, is the synthesis. For example, the poet T.S. Eliot had an almost exact Sun in Libra trine Neptune in Gemini. He aspired to, and delighted in the quest for the eternal realities. His work is full of Sun–Neptune imagery, as in *The Four Quartets*:

> The river is within us, the sea is all about us
> For most of us, there is only the unattended
> Moment, the moment in and out of time

THE SQUARE

Four is the product of 2 × 2. It is two to the power of two. It is therefore very much to do with making things manifest and the exercise of the will. It is related to challenge and effort and the need 'to get to grips with' the planetary principles involved. It produces restless striving, but, since the two planets are at right angles to each other, it can also mean that the two actors 'go off at a tangent' to each other, or block each other's expression.

Jung was born with the Sun in an almost exact outgoing square to Neptune. He was challenged by the need to integrate (Sun) the unconscious (Neptune) into his life path (Sun). This led him to focus (Sun) much of his life's effort (square) on Neptunian matters such as dreams, myths, alchemy, mysticism, and the process of making this personal (Sun). It also produced a major crisis when he went into a state of psychosis, and personal identity (Sun) was nearly swamped out by collective issues (Neptune). It also meant that he could at times be vague and unreliable.

THE QUINTILE

Although referred to in older textbooks as a 'minor' aspect, the division of the 360° of the circle by five = 72°, the quintile aspect, and its multiple of 144°, the bi-quintile, is of primary importance. Five is the number of consciousness and choice. It represents the creative power of we human beings to shape our own life according to our own understanding and intentions. Martin Luther King had his Sun exactly 144° Neptune. This is the signature of someone who will consciously aspire to focus (Sun) their own life around some kind of vision or dream (Neptune). When King said 'I have a dream' he was speaking from his visionary heart. The downside of such an intimate union with Neptune can be a lack of personal boundaries, so that, for example, it is now known that King copied a substantial part of his doctoral thesis from an unacknowl-edged source.

THE SEXTILE

The endlessly busy worker bee creating its hexagonal honey-comb is a perfect symbol of the number six, which as 2×3 is the objective expression, two, of the life principle, three. The sextile combines both the life, vitality and motivation of three-ness with the manifesting, objectifying qualities of two-ness. Hence it is motivated activity: busy-ness, business, business-like. It encourages a working relationship between the planets and angles involved. It is the practical idealist. Jean-Jacques Rousseau, the philosopher, was born with the outgoing sextile, as was Arthur Koestler who worked on a kibbutz, became a dedicated (Sun) communist (Neptune), had a mystical experi-ence (Sun-Neptune) and went on to espouse the integration (Sun) of a transcendent dimension (Neptune) into everyday thought. His last years were spent actively campaigning for euthanasia, the voluntary (Sun) dissolution (Neptune) of the individual.

THE SEPTILE

Before the days of the computer, the septile series of aspects of 51° 26′, the ⅐th part of the 360° zodiac circle, were almost impossible to see in the chart and so were ignored or classed as 'minor' aspects. In fact, the division by seven is one of the most powerful of all. This is not surprising as from earliest times the number seven has always been considered to be of supreme importance. The Bible tells us that the world was created in seven days, and of course the whole world still runs on a seven-day week. And in most languages the seven days are named after the seven planets. The seven series of aspects relate to inspiration, and being captured by the imaginative

and mystical. George Harrison, the most mystical of the Beatles, has Sun bi-septile Neptune.

THE SEMI-SQUARE AND SESQUIQUADRATE

The division by eight = 2 × 2 × 2 gives 2 cubed, an aspect of 45°. Eight is the number of concrete manifestation, of real substance. This aspect and the aspect of 135 = 3 × 45 are to do with productive effort. The astrologer, idealist philosopher and mystic John Addey, the visionary founder of both the Astrological Association and the Urania Trust, had Sun semi-square a rising Neptune.

THE NONILE

The division by nine gives an aspect of 40°. Nine is 3 × 3, the delight of delight, and is related to the higher ideals which guide us and motivate us. The planets joined by a nine-based aspect will feature strongly in the ideals of the individual. Sun–Neptune connected on the ninth harmonic suggests an essential altruism. This is the picture of the idealistic and visionary (Neptune) leader (Sun). Paddy Ashdown, leader of the Liberal Democrats in the UK, and President Clinton both have this contact as does businessman Richard Branson.

THE DECILE

The division by 10 is an aspect of 36° and the ³⁄₁₀ is 108°. The number 10, like the 10th house and 10th sign Capricorn, is very much associated with the career and profession, and special talents. Planets linked by decile work together to produce real knowledge (5) that can be expressed in the world and in a vocation. David Copperfield, the hugely successful professional illusionist and stage magician, has Sun–36–Neptune, a classic case of someone who 'knows how to create an illusion'.

Twelve is 3×4. It is a combination of aspiration (3) and effort (4), so a sometimes awkward but potentially fertile mixture of trine and square. Twelve is the number most related to the unfoldment of life. The division of the circle of the zodiac by 12 gives 12 30° segments of the zodiac. But when one planet is 30° from another they are in very different signs. This often makes for an awkward but potentially powerful conversation, which wants to be relaxed (3) but feels compelled to take action (4). Dustin Hoffman was born with Sun in Leo, sign of the show-man who seeks to be centre stage, 30° from Neptune, and the Moon in Virgo, sign of the self-effacing perfectionist. Here the Sun, the capacity to be and to project oneself, is linked in this delighting, striving aspect with sensitive, imaginative Neptune, god of dreams, illusions and the theatre. The whole of Hoffman's professional career has expressed a tension between these poles. His meticulous research, submerging himself in the image of another in order that he may shine, can be witnessed in his portrayal of the autistic brother in *The Rainman*. This imaginative dichotomy is most explicitly expressed in *Tootsie*, his self-mocking portrayal of the self-important, pretentious out-of-work actor who dresses up as the lovable, gentle 'real woman' Dorothy in order to get a part in a soap opera. The star who is not what they seem: a pure Sun–Neptune dance.

THE QUINCUNX

$150° = 5 \times 30°$, combines 3, 4 and 5. The quincunx is a more conscious (5) version of the semi-sextile. It can be a very powerful contact, but it can produce a certain 'divine discontent' and unease between the factors involved, which demands their conscious reconciliation. Jeffrey Archer, the politician, bestseller writer and former bankrupt, has Sun–150–Neptune. He both aspires to be a charismatic leader, yet is also a romantic.

His enormous success as he worked creatively with his Neptune contrasts sharply with his earlier failure which put him 'all at sea'.

LUNAR ASPECTS

The Moon in the chart speaks of our natural, spontaneous relationship and approach to the world. Her aspects will show the gods with whom she is on familiar terms and which will in consequence colour the individual's gut-level response to life. So, for example, if the Moon aspects Neptune there will be heightened sensitivity and imagination and a tendency to idealize and dream. If at the same time there is an aspect to Mars, it is likely that such ideals and dreams can be translated into action.

SOLAR ASPECTS

Planets in aspect to the Sun will normally feature clearly in the characteristic way in which we organize our life; the way we make decisions and make up our mind. Planets aspecting the Sun can be seen as the close colleagues which the hero will need to work with in order to attain the goal of self-realization.

UNASPECTED PLANETS

It has been found that when a planet has no major aspects, it can often be very 'pure' in its expression. However, its activity, not being especially connected with the rest of the chart, can be either all switched on or all switched off.

Conversations are not necessarily just two-way. Many characters can be engaged in the dialogue, and often are. Mercury, for example, may be aspected to Saturn, giving a demand for clarity and discipline to the thoughts and a somewhat conventional, practical, orthodox mind. Yet at the same time it may also be closely aspected to Neptune, stimulating the imagination and the ability to identify intuitively with others and an ability to communicate myths and fairy tales. Such a paradoxical combination can produce someone who is able to work professionally (Mercury–Saturn) with dreams (Mercury–Neptune), who is able to write and communicate clearly about intangible and normally elusive subjects.

MID-POINTS

An especially powerful form of aspect is when one factor in the birth chart stands half-way between two others, i.e. on their mid-point, or in square or semi-square to the mid-point within an orb of about 1° 30′. This pattern acts like a triple conjunction with the factor in the middle bringing together the ideas of the two on either side. Thus, for example, Freud has his Sun, the very focus of his life, exactly conjunct the mid-point of Mercury (mind) and Pluto (the Underworld), a combination that speaks vividly of depth psychology. Carl Jung, his pupil and close colleague who developed his ideas, likewise has the Sun with Mercury–Pluto; in his case it is semi-square the mid-point. Continuing the Sun–Neptune theme above, some individuals who had Neptune in aspect to the Sun–Moon mid-point, thereby placing Neptune at the heart of their lives, include Jacques Cousteau, the great underwater explorer, Leggs Diamond, the gangster who made a fortune peddling alcohol during prohibition, and St Teresa of Avila, the great exponent of mystical prayer and contemplation. In each case a totally Neptunian life, but at very different levels of expression!

Mid-point relationships are often impossible to see with the unaided eye but can be instantly identified by the computer which can set all the information out in a readily digestible form.

LUCKY NUMBERS? – HARMONIC CHARTS

Lucky numbers can be pure superstition, yet each of us tends to be more at home with some numbers than others. In these days of computers it is possible to look at the way in which a chart is resonating with each of the numbers. By getting the computer to multiply the natal chart by the number under consideration creates a harmonic chart is created. This shows in what way the planets and angles are brought together by this number. This is an extremely powerful technique for arriving at the working of the number archetypes within the individual. The use of such charts was developed by John Addey in the 1960s. Charles Harvey then went on to discover that these methods had in fact been used for hundreds of years in Hindu astrology. This powerful technique for studying hidden aspect patterns is explored in the books *Harmonic Charts* and *Working with Astrology (see Bibliography)*.

RULING PLANETS

As we saw in Chapter 4, each planet 'rules' a particular sign or signs. So, for example, the Sun is said to rule the sign of Leo. This means that there is always a connection between the Sun in a chart and the house in the chart where the sign Leo is found. So if Leo is on the cusp of the seventh house, and the Sun in the chart is in Sagittarius in the tenth house, the person will not only find themselves drawn into partnership with Leo types but probably individuals who are high-profile (Sun in tenth) adventurous explorers (Sagittarius) of some kind. Aspects to the Sun will further colour the picture in this case. Whilst the ruler of each house is important, a special emphasis is normally accorded to the planet which rules the rising sign. This is normally considered to be the ruling planet of the chart as a whole.

The way in which the planets talk with one another is subtle and various, but the more precisely and attentively we listen, the greater understanding we will have of the profound potential their geometries can provide.

THE CIRCULAR
ADVENTURE
– THE SIGNS OF THE ZODIAC

Know that you are another world in miniature and have in you
Sol and Luna and even the stars.

ORIGEN

The earth looked at from Heaven is like a ball with twelve leath-
ern stripes, each in a different colour...

PLATO *THE TIMAEUS*

When the astrologer studies a horoscope, he or she is looking at a map of a unique combination of four essential components. The planets represent psychological urges or functions – different kinds of energies and needs – or we might think of them as the main characters in an individual life drama, the entity or 'god' that invokes the action. The signs indicate the way in which a planetary energy will tend to express itself; the signs modulate planetary expression by giving the background themes of the drama and the unique qualities or ways of being. The houses locate the action in specific areas of life, such as home, career and relationships. And the aspects articulate the story line through planetary relationships: this is the inner dialogue – the planets 'speaking with each other' – that fuels the individual story and manifests through the talents, strengths, weaknesses, conflicts and aspirations which lie within and drive an individual's life drama.

THE BUILDING BLOCKS

The 12-fold circle of the zodiac contains within it some obvious geometrical truths of nature: there are four elements – Fire, Earth, Air and Water – and three modes of expression or phases of operation – Cardinal, Fixed and Mutable. Cardinal energy has an initiating quality; when the Sun enters the Cardinal signs (Aries, Cancer, Libra, Capricorn), a definite shift occurs: a new season begins. Fixed energy has a consolidating and maintaining quality; each season comes to its fullest expression when the Sun travels through these signs (Taurus, Leo, Scorpio, Aquarius). Mutable energy has a disseminating quality; as the Sun moves through these signs (Gemini, Virgo, Sagittarius, Pisces) we can feel that change is in the air and the seasons are making way for a new phase. Each group of three signs of the same element is termed a Triplicity; and each group of four signs of the same mode or quality is termed a Quadruplicity. But before we look at the zodiac signs in more detail, a word about typology, or the science of categorizing human nature.

The idea of typology, or classifying people according to different qualities, goes back a long way. The ancient Greek philosopher Empedocles was one of the originators of the view that the universe is made up of fire, earth, air and water. Medieval thinkers applied this idea further in their recognition of four basic temperaments based on the theory of the 'humours' in the blood: the choleric (fiery) type, the melancholic (earthy) type, the sanguine (airy) type, and the phlegmatic (watery) type. The Swiss psychologist Carl Jung continued these observations this century with a more sophisticated psychological lens, to show

that people apparently do tend to operate in life according to one or two dominant functions. Jung's four classifications link up exactly with the four medieval types, and he postulates them as intuition (the fiery type), sensation (the earthy type), thinking (the airy type) and feeling (the watery type). Different cultures throughout the centuries have categorized human beings according to different values and viewpoints, but always and everywhere underlying our predisposition to categorize is the awareness and fascination about difference and sameness.

Generally speaking, most people don't like being 'classified' because it feels like an insult to one's uniqueness. But uniqueness, or rather, a truly actualized individuality, does not come with the mere fact of being born. We are potential individuals – individuals in the making. The fact that people can be 'grouped' does not deny uniqueness; rather, it affirms the fact that we inherently share certain characteristics with others, that we have strengths and weaknesses to work with, and – most importantly – that not everybody is the same as us. What is also important to understand is that each of us has all the elements (or psychological functions if we are equating with Jung's four typologies) within us, regardless of the fact that we feel most confident using only one or two of them most of the time. The development of our unique individuality demands that we take a closer look at the least familiar or 'evolved' bits of ourselves – and astrology is one of the ancient disciplines that can help us do that.

The four elements are of special interest to astrologers for each one represents a distinct way of viewing, approaching, evaluating and interpreting life. The four elements (and the twelve signs) are also classified according to the most basic of all polarities: yin and yang, feminine and masculine, negative and positive. The yin elements and signs are more passive, introverted, contained, self-reflective, whilst the yang elements and signs are more active, extroverted, outwardly dynamic and assertive. The planets feel more or less at home in different elements; that is, their energies will be moderated and expressed according to the element (and sign) they occupy in the birth chart. The elements are allocated in an orderly sequence around the zodiac, starting with the fire sign Aries and repeating the pattern fire, earth, air, water, three times, as seen in Figure 6.1.

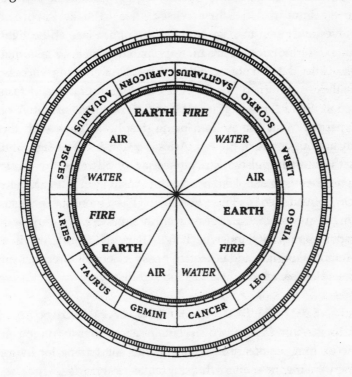

Figure 6.1. The signs of the zodiac and their elements.

Fire is the most 'yang' of the two masculine or positive elements. It illumines and transforms; it burns and is unpredictable, unstable, but also warming, exciting and creative. A fiery temperament is essentially positive, extrovert, pushing ahead into life, and motivating others through the sheer force of charismatic confidence. A strongly fire type tends to be demonstrative, dramatic, intense. These individuals have a strong intuitive side: they 'sense' when to make important moves and often manage to be in the right place at the right time. Fire individuals are more prepared to risk, to take that leap into the unknown; either they are a 'roaring success' or they 'get burned' by the excesses of enthusiasm and rash action. Fire's 'knowing' is not a logical one; it is an intuitive experience that comes from being deeply in touch with the mysterious centre of the self. Aries is a Cardinal Fire sign, and is the most impulsive and pioneering of all three fire signs: spontaneous, outspoken, headstrong, rushing in where angels fear to tread. Leo is a Fixed Fire sign: it has a more stable, regal, kingly quality that manifests well in situations where power and responsibility must be handled wisely. Sagittarius is a Mutable Fire sign, and is keen to fire sparks in all directions on its endless search for meaning and self-discovery.

EARTH – TAURUS, VIRGO, CAPRICORN

Earth is a 'yin' element which contains and brings to fruition all the exciting visions of fire. Earth is our solid arena for living and working; no matter what our fantasies and wishes may be, we must stay 'grounded' in reality – in the realm of what is possible – if we are to perform at all. Earth is the most stable of the elements, and therefore the earthy individual tends to be practical, sensible, conservative, dependable, capable of running a business or household efficiently and making things grow.

From Jung's perspective, this is the sensation type who approaches life according to material reality: how does it act, taste, feel, measure up in the 'real' world? But if an earthy individual lacks fire, then passivity and lack of vision may become a barrier to expanding beyond their known, quantifiable and controllable universe. The earthy type can then be narrow, pedantic, sluggish, obstinate. Fire and Earth make a creative partnership, even though their natures seem fundamentally alien to each other. Taurus is a Fixed Earth sign and is sensual, determined and patient, but also profoundly stubborn when a challenge to the status quo threatens its security. Virgo is a Mutable Earth sign. Virgo's approach is to analyse the material world and organize things into logical, efficient routines, always with the intention to improve and streamline the status quo. Capricorn is a Cardinal Earth sign. This approach to life is a very ambitious, aspiring one, although Capricorn can sometimes value tradition and conformity to the exclusion of the innovation that keeps life moving forward.

AIR – GEMINI, LIBRA, AQUARIUS

Air, although not as unstable and assertive as Fire, is also an extroverted and animated 'yang' element. Air is the all-pervasive element that connects us all through our constantly moving atmosphere. This is the thinking type who seeks the rational principle at work within the operations of nature and human behaviour. Clear, objective reasoning is the great strength of airy individuals, as is their capacity for lively communication. The airy temperament is gregarious but civilized, curious but co-operative, intellectual but casual and often witty, fun-loving and sociable. Although airy individuals enjoy being with others, their interactions have a distinctly impersonal quality. As the all-encompassing element of air might suggest, the airy type likes the extensive experience rather than the

intensely intimate encounter. Airy types can rationalize away their discomfort with feelings; but what they lack in emotional commitment they make up for with diplomatic friendliness. Gemini is a Mutable Air sign and loves to sample the amazing variety of people and experiences with a childlike *joie de vivre*. Libra is a Cardinal Air sign and seeks justice and ideal harmony by balancing its views against many others. Aquarius is a Fixed Air sign and is interested in ideologies that affect humanity. It shares its understanding with friends and is devoted to the common good.

WATER – CANCER, SCORPIO, PISCES

Water is the most mysterious and 'yin' of the elements. It is cooling, refreshing and nurturing like the spring rain; it can be mysterious and forbidding like the deep blue sea, and also overwhelming and engulfing as in the terror of a flood. Whilst the heat of fire rises, air moves constantly in a steady circling of the earth, and earth slumbers in stillness, water is either contained by its boundaries or penetrates down to the roots. This shows how water is symbolic of empathy and feeling. Water represents our need to merge, to connect at a deep, emotional level; and indeed this element equates with the feeling function in Jung's typologies. The watery individual is sympathetic and romantic, often governed by mysterious, unfathomable moods. Watery types will often ask 'does this feel right?' even though they may not be able to explain their gut reactions in a logical way. Very often this type has a pronounced psychic sensitivity because a very fundamental part of them is 'plugged' into the deep, watery matrix that contains us all. Cancer is a Cardinal Water sign and is very cautious but desirous of inclusion and intimacy; it has a tenacious maternal streak and maintains a strong emotional tie with loved ones and with the past. Scorpio is a Fixed Water sign and feels all emotions very intensely.

Scorpio operates from a powerful connection with basic instincts and therefore is unafraid of facing the darker human emotions. Pisces is a Mutable Water sign and can easily identify with the whole spectrum of human emotion. Pisces is highly imaginative, chameleon-like, and compassionate.

THE ZODIAC SIGNS

The zodiac circle – the path of the Earth's circumambulation around the Sun – was described by the early 20th-century astrologer Alan Leo as the 'Earth's aura', and as the Earth's 'vitasphere' by the late astrologer Grant Lewi. In other words, the zodiac represents the collective cosmic environment in which the Earth moves and has its being. Each individual living on the Earth is a cell within that collective body and has a unique relationship to the collective. The zodiac, then, is a 12-fold pattern of life experience: each sign symbolizes a vital phase of life, an archetypal segment of the whole, as well as a basic personality type. It should be remembered, however, that there is no personality woven from one thread alone and that every person contains all 12 signs – but in different ways and varying combinations. The inner logic of the signs also expresses itself through a correspondence with the human body. The ancient maxim 'as above, so below' informs this internal logic, so that we begin to see the wholeness of the greater 'cosmic being' and the wholeness of man's individual being reflected in one another through the symbolism of the zodiac.

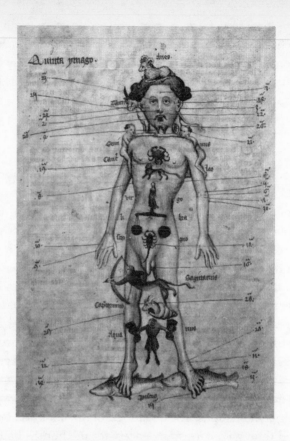

Figure 6.2. This 17th-century woodcut shows the correspondences between the parts of the body and the signs of the zodiac. Aries the Ram rules the head. Taurus the Bull rules the throat and neck. Gemini the Twins rules the lungs, arms and hands. Cancer the crab rules the breast and stomach. Leo the Lion rules the heart and spine. Virgo the Virgin rules the digestive system. Libra the Scales rules the kidneys. Scorpio the Scorpion rules the genitals and excretory system. Sagittarius the Archer rules the thighs. Capricorn the goat rules the knees and skeletal system. Aquarius the Water Bearer rules the lower legs and circulation. Pisces the Fish rules the feet.

PRINCIPLES OF ASTROLOGY

ARIES

THE SUN PASSES THROUGH ARIES BETWEEN ABOUT 21 MARCH–19 APRIL.

Aries is a positive, Cardinal Fire sign and the one that begins the zodiac with the start of spring. This is the thrusting, raw energy that conquers the cold winter sleep, and this quality is reflected in the Arian instinct for action and leadership. Ruled by Mars, the god of war and competition, Aries is daring, impulsive, enterprising, sometimes foolhardy, but always optimistic. Aries is represented by the ram, and in ancient Egypt it was the ram-headed god Ammon who stood for the primitive, self-engendering, creative energy of the world. Bold, dynamic, assertive, the Aries individual, whether male or female, has a distinctly masculine creative drive which takes them into the battle of life with great expectancy. Aries is competitive, restless and independent, desiring immediacy and scope for experiencing their ingenuity and skill. The inner need of Aries is to conquer – either a mythical ogre who threatens something beautiful and fragile, or to conquer fears within themselves. In all their activities, the Aries personality is building – and eager to experience – a core sense of self; that is the great adventure of

life. For the Aries individual, this core self consists of repeated experiences of successfully 'doing', building up skills and knowledge that give them mastery over existence. These individuals want to feel that they can affect their world. As the sign associated with archetypal beginnings, Aries loves to initiate. Not given to wasting time quibbling over bureaucratic details, Aries pushes ahead with 'what matters' and is not worried about the mistakes that could be made through rash action. Not surprisingly, impatience and recklessness are Aries' Achilles heel. So is the tendency to ride roughshod over their more fragile, needy feelings. Aries loves a difficult challenge and gets bored with too much self-reflection. Aries' virtue is innate optimism, a positive belief in its abilities to master problems, and an inability to hold a grudge. There is a naivety and vulnerability about Aries that is often hidden underneath a brusque exterior. This may also manifest as an innocence which makes them prey to more cunning types. Aries is loyal and passionately devoted to family and loved ones, although they will always need freedom to pursue their own career and interests. Planets in Aries will express their energies in a bold, enthusiastic, honest way. If Aries is strongly emphasized in your birth chart, much of your life will tend to focus on defining your identity, learning how to assert your will, and achieving recognition for your unique personal characteristics. The double-Aries poet Algernon Swinburne expressed the Arian thrill of 'doing' in this line from 'The Hymn to Man':

Glory to Man in the highest! for Man is the master of things.

Aries rules the head and its motto is 'I am'.

TAURUS

THE SUN PASSES THROUGH TAURUS BETWEEN
ABOUT 20 APRIL–20 MAY.

Taurus is a negative (or 'yin') Fixed Earth sign and represents the solid containing element that nurtures, stabilizes and brings to fruition all of nature's creative potency. The bull is the ancient symbol of Taurus which has universally represented the strength and passion of the earthy, instinctual realm. During the month of May, ancient fertility rites honoured the prolificness and feminine power of the Earth Mother. Taurus is ruled by Venus, the goddess of love and beauty. The Taurean phase of the year is a time of sensual beauty when new colours and vibrant scents pervade the world; no one wants to hurry in the warm, spring sunshine and we can 'get drunk' on the luxuriant beauty of nature. The fiery energy of Aries is now grounded and life begins to relax and unfold; the Taurean individual registers the beauty of nature with his senses and slows down to enjoy it all. Remember Ferdinand the Bull sitting amidst the daisies? We can begin to get a feel for the Taurean personality: sensual, easy-going, a lover of beauty and good food, very much in touch with the body and the gratification of basic needs. Emotionally demonstrative and mentally pragmatic, Taureans make good organizers, teachers, parents – anything that requires care, patience, diligence and down-to-earth common sense. Taureans don't give up or let go easily; they form deep attachments to loved ones, home and possessions, and they can work lovingly and patiently on projects as if they had an infinite amount of time. They tend to distrust anything they cannot touch, taste or measure, and are famous for their extreme obstinacy. Taureans can literally dig in their heels when challenged, so it's best just to present the idea ('plant a seed') and let them come round to a new shift in themselves in their own good time – just as in nature, there is no hurry! But there is also a proneness to getting stuck in a rut, and to resist even seeing other viewpoints and to devaluing the more subtle, imaginal (unseen, symbolic) realms of human endeavour. They can also become very possessive and materialistic, and their occasional over-indulgence can lead to weight problems. Taurean stubbornness can lead to a very constipated, dead-end state of affairs which then invites the cathartic activity of its opposite sign, Scorpio, to encourage an interest in the 'rationally unexplainable' and a desire for regeneration. Venus-ruled Taureans are often very musical and artistic, and display a bawdy sense of humour. Planets in Taurus will express their energies in a calm, earthy, determined way. If Taurus is strongly emphasized in your birth chart, much of your life may focus on substantiating your identity through work, building a solid material base, and enjoying the pleasures of the natural world. The Taurean composer Irving Berlin wrote a song that sums up what Taureans love best: 'Doing what comes naturally'. Taurus rules the throat and neck, and its motto is 'I possess'.

GEMINI

THE SUN PASSES THROUGH GEMINI BETWEEN ABOUT 21 MAY–20 JUNE.

Gemini is a positive, Mutable Air sign which takes us into a transition phase of the year: 'flaming June' with its endless variety of colours and restless bees and butterflies. Deep Taurean stability gives way to versatility and change, and Gemini is the first sign to rationally perceive the rich spectrum of life forms to be found in the environment. In mythology, the story of the famous twins Castor and Pollux exemplifies the essentially dual nature of this sign: one twin is a mortal, the other dwells with the gods, and this sibling separation brings both agony and fascination as the twins meet up now and then to compare notes. Studying the fascinating dualities in people and in all aspects of life is something this sign loves to do. Gemini is ruled by Mercury, the ancient god of the intellect and swift communication, which makes this sign a natural communicator, teacher, writer and go-between. Gemini excels at making connections between apparently disparate subjects and people. They can zoom in with insights and witticisms which contain just enough truth to get more stodgy types thinking, and then they're off again. Like the restless butterfly, Gemini does not want to dwell long on ponderous details. In general, Gemini hates two things: boredom and emotional displays. Geminian energy is notoriously asexual and amoral: examining information from all sides and with a sharp mercurial objectivity gives them the right (they believe!) to contradict themselves many times, if necessary, in order to satisfy curiosity. This is the work of Hermes who dwells forever on the boundaries, linking opposites in unexpected ways. Geminian energy requires mobility and space for experimentation; it is playful, searching, sociable, perceptive, categorizing, refreshing, insightful and sometimes annoyingly irresponsible. Being so 'cerebral', Gemini finds it difficult relating to its emotional needs and so may unwittingly employ double standards in order to get emotional needs met. Gemini can easily skim the surface of life, and easily gets bored. This is the Peter Pan of the zodiac, forever resisting the commitment of adulthood, forever keeping all options open. If it is ever to embrace the richness of the inner Gemini paradox, Gemini must delve into its darker side – the other twin. Planets in Gemini will express their energies in an alert, restless, rational way. If Gemini is strongly emphasized in your birth chart, you will always need variety and stimulation, and much of your life path will focus on the development of mental concentration and verbal and written communication. The actor John Barrymore was a Gemini and succinctly expressed the Geminian duality and wit:

> One of my chief regrets during my years in the theatre is that I couldn't sit in the audience and watch me.

Gemini rules the arms and hands, and its motto is 'I communicate'.

CANCER

THE SUN PASSES THROUGH CANCER BETWEEN
ABOUT 21 JUNE–22 JULY

Cancer is a negative, Cardinal Water sign which marks the beginning of summer, the time of the Sun's maximum strength. We know Cancer's symbol as the crab, but in ancient Egyptian times the scarab or dung beetle was associated with this sign. The scarab's eggs grew in a ball of dung, and for the Egyptians this was a spiritual symbol showing the mysterious process of incarnating life. As the first water sign of the zodiac, Cancer represents the great ocean of life and the emotional bonds which link us to a nuclear family, to a specific past, and because of these roots, also to the future. But the crab is a creature of both sea and land, and this shows the predilection for Cancer-ian individuals to partake of both watery, imaginative depths as well as the secure homes into which they scuttle when danger appears. The Cancerian's defences are like the crab's: a crusty exterior protects a vulnerable interior, and they shift and manoeuvre around a problem until, feeling safe enough to ponder and brood upon it, they come up with a shrewd but always fair solution. Ruled by the Moon, Cancerians are very emotional

and their moods wax and wane with an irrational, unfathomable logic. One minute they may be clear-headed, affectionate and helpful, the next minute dreamy or sulking and withdrawn. Like the cycles of the Moon and the tides of the sea, there is an emotional coherence and timing to their feeling states, and when they emerge from a period of mysterious brooding they are at their most creative. Cancerian characteristics include sensitivity, intuition, compassion, devotion, and a deep urge to be needed and appreciated. But Cancer is not only poetic and imaginative; it is also a sign with a shrewd business sense and an ability to understand and work well with the tides of economic change. They often have an uncanny capacity to intuit public sentiment, and so can manipulate or use this talent to good effect in writing, journalism and public affairs. Cancerian energy needs something to nurture and fuss over, like a mother hen. This 'something' can range from a house full of children, to a class of aspiring students, to a growing business or a novel or musical score. Essentially, Cancerians need to feel they are part of something, and that the people or projects they are tending with their emotional energy are developing, growing, thriving, coming alive with the life they have given. Planets in Cancer will express their energies in a sensitive, emotional, cautious way. If Cancer is strongly emphasized in your birth chart, you will seek to understand your emotional links with a living past so that you may best express your place within the family of man. The American songwriter Stephen Foster was a Cancerian who wrote songs that reflected the poignant yearnings of this sign, in particular his famous 'My Old Kentucky Home'. Cancer rules the breast and the stomach, and its motto is 'I belong'.

LEO

THE SUN PASSES THROUGH LEO BETWEEN
ABOUT 23 JULY–22 AUGUST.

Leo is a positive, Fixed Fire sign which corresponds to that phase in the yearly cycle when the sun's rays are most concentrated. Leo's ruling deity is the Sun, the centre and driving force of our solar system. During this period we can feel the sun's force as its fierce radiance embraces the environment in a baking stillness. The creative power of the Sun is symbolized by the kingly lion, a noble and dangerous beast whose rule is thwarted at the peril of any transgressor. In ancient Egypt it was the lion-headed goddess Sekhmet who symbolized the intuitive power and might of the solar deity. Leo is concerned with the unique creative gift of individuality, the need for recognition and respect shown towards that unique selfhood, and the desire to contribute authentically to the larger group. Leo is the hero or heroine who is seeking to fulfil his or her own destiny, and this all-consuming concern often makes them mythologize their life. The solar energy that fuels our solar system is a potent metaphor for this zodiacal phase of human development: the energy source for life is the innermost self, the spiritual essence, and it is felt that contact with this centre ensures that one's life will be not only magnificent, but also one's own. Not unlike the child who has discovered his ability to create, the Leo personality wants to be a centre of light whose warm rays are reflected back in an appreciative glow. This highlights a difference between Leo and the first fire sign Aries, for Leo is acutely aware of its impact on others and needs positive interaction and affirmation; whereas Aries is less needful of social feedback and usually prefers to pursue its goals alone. Leonine energy is loyal, steadfast, and exudes confidence and largesse, but equally it can become dogmatic, arrogant and tyrannical. Strongly Leonine personalities are extremely subjective and self-absorbed and often invite rude reminders from others that the outer world does not revolve around them in the same way it does in their imaginations. But their intense idealism and commitment to the highest in themselves makes them fine leaders and organizers; their innate understanding of myth and drama very often draws them to professions involved with the theatre. Leo needs a big canvas on which to splash, play and mould the meaning of his or her life. Without that personal meaning, life is simply not worth living for this kingly, radiant beast. Planets in Leo will express their energies in a wholehearted and authoritative way. If you have Leo strongly emphasized in your chart, much of your life will focus on expressing the radiance of your unique self and gaining recognition for your contribution to the collective. Theologian Gerard Manley Hopkins expressed a Leonine perception when he said that 'the world is charged with the grandeur of God'. Leo rules the heart, and its motto is 'I create'.

VIRGO

THE SUN PASSES THROUGH VIRGO BETWEEN
ABOUT 23 AUGUST–23 SEPTEMBER.

Virgo is a negative, Mutable Earth sign whose place in the zodiacal cycle signifies another transition phase. Virgo in Latin means 'virgin' and indeed the maiden or virgin goddess is the mascot of the sixth sign. Virgin in this sense means 'sufficient unto oneself', or not depending on any other being or deity for one's purpose or wellbeing. The essence of Virgo is linked with the sacred integrity of the earth itself, and the intelligent laws of nature which, when respected by humans, allow us to cultivate and enjoy a wide variety of plants and herbs with nutritional, healing powers. This highlights the energy of Virgo's astrological ruler, Mercury, the god of intellect and intelligent co-ordination. Whereas Taurus, the first Earth sign, represents the deep fecundity and power of the earth, Virgo exemplifies the efficiency of earth and the delicate sophistication of the web of life when Nature's laws are respected and applied. The Virgo personality expresses this principle in the need to be usefully engaged with his or her environment, and in order to do this Virgo will study, acquire knowledge and master the skills necessary to lead a useful, productive life. Virgoan qualities include quiet ingenuity, a desire to serve and to improve, versatility, analytical and critical thinking, self-doubt, modesty and self-sufficiency. In contrast to Leo's need for recognition, Virgo's deepest satisfaction comes from knowing he or she has done a job well. Further, in terms of Virgo's relationship to the kingly sign that precedes it, Virgo's role is to take the fiery essence of 'self' and refine it and consecrate it in service to their world. This Virgoan tendency to work hard in order to improve can make this individual very serious and self-critical: perfectionism is their aspiration and Achilles heel. Over-identification with work and obsessive perfectionism can create irritability and health problems, and often Virgo has to learn to take time out for frivolous enjoyment – something that does not come easy to this sign. Virgoan energy is discriminating and ordering, and there is a love of classification and system, and consequently a fear of chaos when things don't go to plan. Being adept at ordering, categorizing and serving, Virgo is attracted to roles involving organization, practical analysis, and often health care. But this same talent for precise focus and practical skill also makes Virgo an exceptionally fine craftsman and artist. Planets in Virgo will express their energies in a practical and conscientious way. If Virgo is strongly emphasized in your chart, to a large extent your life will focus on making the daily round a ritual of service, on streamlining your talents, and mastering skills which bring greater efficiency and enjoyment in work. Count Tolstoy (both Sun and Moon in Virgo) expressed an archetypal Virgoan sentiment when he said:

> The happiness of man consists in life, and life is in labour … the vocation of every man and woman is to serve other people.

Virgo rules the digestive system and its motto is 'I perfect and serve'.

LIBRA

The illustrations used in this chapter are 15th century symbols of the zodiac as presented in *Poeticon Astronomicon de Mundi et Sphaera* (1482). That the glyphs for Scorpio and Libra, the Scorpion and the Scales, are joined is testimony to an ancient legend about these two signs once being represented by a single figure. This imagery relates to the constellations of these signs rather than to the tropical zodiac. Libra has been called 'chelae' or 'claws of the scorpion', or we can imagine that Scorpio's emotional intensity is a reaction to the balance and rational objectiv-ity of Libra.

THE SUN PASSES THROUGH LIBRA BETWEEN
ABOUT 24 SEPTEMBER–23 OCTOBER

Libra is a positive Cardinal Air sign and, like Aries, its opposite sign, it ushers in the time of equinoctial balance. But whilst Aries gives birth to the new life of spring, Libra offers thanks-giving for the beauty and harvest which is reaped in the autumn as the yearly cycle of nature is nearing its end. Libra is ruled by Venus, the planet of harmony, social relationships and etiquette, love and beauty. In Egyptian mythology the goddess Maat represents this Libran principle: her activity was to weigh the hearts of the dead on the scales of truth; if there was proper balance, the soul could continue on its journey into eternity. It is this ideal balance in all things to which Libra aspires which is why one of their dominant qualities is idealism. Librans value equality and justice, and yet to achieve this end – to redress an imbalance – they may go to great lengths. An example of this is the Libran Conservative Prime Minister Margaret Thatcher who sought to rectify political and economic imbalances that had come about through many years of socialist governments. Another famous Libran political activist whose role was to fight extreme social injustice was Lech Walesa, the Polish trade unionist. Librans may be sweet-tempered and generally easy-going, but that belies the feistiness that lies beneath the surface and which likes to stir things up in relationships in order to get a response, in order to find out what step of the social dance everyone's – including their own – foot happens to be in. Libra's glyph can be seen as a setting sun, indicating that at this point in the zodiacal cycle all that has gone before to build an individual self (Aries through Virgo) must now be taken out into the world to meet the 'other' and to know itself in the world. Librans tend to be interested in people and often become very adept at managing people and getting the best out of them. In fact, Librans have a strong need to relate to others, to be in dialogue with an important 'other', for this is the way they find out who they are and what they think and feel. Libra's need for others makes them more dependent than they appear, but Libra's instinct is always to define themselves in relation to an-'other'. Trying to consider many different view-points can make Libra chronically indecisive, and the need to keep the peace frequently forces others to respond with firm-ness, even anger. Being an air sign, Libra prefers to rationally observe and discuss in an appropriate, respectful, civilized manner. Their idealism may take them into law and politics where they can pursue and, as in the case of Walesa, even fight for the ideals they believe in. Librans seek to communicate and may also express their creative struggle with dualistic paradoxes (self and other, male and female, good and evil, light and dark) through literature, theatre and art. Planets in Libra will express their energies in a civilized, considered, co-operative way. If Libra is strongly emphasized in your chart, you will invest a great deal of personal energy in the dynamics of friendships and relationships, and these will be both a challenge and a source of great nourishment as you struggle to define yourself. Oscar Wilde expressed characteristic Libran style and wit, and one quote for which he is well known reveals his Libran insistence on mannerisms and social comportment:

> It is absurd to divide people into good and bad. People are either
> charming or tedious.

Libra rules the kidneys, and its motto is 'I balance'.

SCORPIO

THE SUN PASSES THROUGH SCORPIO BETWEEN ABOUT 23 OCTOBER–21 NOVEMBER.

Scorpio is a negative Fixed Water sign whose phase in the year in the northern hemisphere corresponds with the decrease of sunlight and the decaying of nature. The connection of this sign with the revivifying powers of matter is crucial to understanding its mysterious essence. Scorpio's ancient ruler, Mars, symbolizes willpower and combative strength, something Scorpio has in abundance. But since the discovery of Pluto, observations have shown that this planet has a more obvious affinity with the secretive and regenerative side of Scorpio, a sign which is known for its intense feeling nature and its unshakeable determination to achieve self-mastery. Scorpio's mascot is the scorpion, a creature of the night which will attack itself when cornered. Although this reflects Scorpio's instinct to retaliate, it also signifies Scorpio's extreme willpower and ability to survive life's most dangerous and painful experiences. Scorpio has another mascot, too – the eagle, a bird of great ferocity and strength. It symbolizes Scorpio's potential to overcome negative emotions and self-destructive tendencies. Scorpio is intensely emotional and powerfully aware of the more primitive emotions of human nature. Most notable of the many ancient myths that involve creatures of the 'dark mother' is the poisonous nine-headed hydra that lives in a dark, swampy cave. This is an image of the power of instinctual life and the danger man risks in denying or repressing it. Scorpio grapples with this side of reality, and strives to develop the emotional courage to look at the darker side of life in order *not* to be deprived of the whole truth. And whatever 'hydra' is found within the human psyche, Scorpio has the courage and wisdom to confront it so that ultimately it can be healed and regenerated. Just as the decaying mulch of autumn leaves eventually enriches the soil, Scorpio senses the hidden capacity for new life and usefulness in the rejected and maimed souls of humanity. Scorpio's intensity can be experienced by others as demanding and overwhelming. All the same, this is their gift: they magnify emotions because they know that emotional truth is the hardest – and the most important – part of being human. Because they feel so intensely, they also have a fear of being controlled, and this gives rise to their secretiveness and mysterious charisma. But equal to their self-protection is their extraordinary commitment and devotion to those they love. Because their traits are underpinned by such intensity of feeling, their negative characteristics appear excessive: possessive, revengeful, manipulative. But when they turn their exacting gaze on themselves, their courageous honesty and perceptiveness pays off for they thrive on the discovery of their hidden depth. Their fascination with human nature and power often takes them into medicine, psychology and politics. Although often silent, seemingly cynical, and not apparently prepossessing to meet at first, when they engage intimately with others, or find themselves in a confrontation, all their passions take over and they

will fight 'to the death' for something in which they believe. Hilary Clinton is a classic Scorpio who puts up a fierce fight for her beliefs as well as her position, even if it requires her to endure the sexual intrigues of her husband. As a water sign, Scorpio is painfully aware of human vulnerability and therefore of the need to protect the defenceless and to avenge abusers. Planets in Scorpio will express their energies in a guarded but persistent way. If Scorpio is strongly emphasized in your birth chart, you will seek to probe and understand the intensities of human relationships and the complexities of the human appetite. Bram Stoker (a double Scorpio), the author of *Dracula*, expressed Scorpionic themes in his work; the following quote, taken from that novel, gives a clear hint:

> Ah, sir, you dwellers in the city cannot enter into the feelings of the hunter.

Scorpio rules the genitals and excretory system, and its motto is 'I regenerate'.

SAGITTARIUS

THE SUN PASSES THROUGH SAGITTARIUS BETWEEN ABOUT 22 NOVEMBER–21 DECEMBER.

Sagittarius is a positive Mutable Fire sign whose symbol is the half-man half-horse centaur clutching his bow and arrow and aiming towards some distant goal. Zeus, the great god of Olympus, presides over this sign through the embodiment of the planet Jupiter. Zeus was called 'the father of gods and men'; this conveys Sagittarius's very masculine type of creativity and an emphasis on the activity of intellect. One unforgettable facet of Zeus is his predilection for pursuing many paramours. This is an image of his prolific creativity and it is this that underpins the identity of this individual: the sense that he or she can pursue what at one point feels like the impossible and move forward into more exciting, more meaningful horizons. Sagittarius is full of aspirations, and the journey of turning them into reality is what they enjoy most. This questing impulse makes them great travellers, for there is a deep love of learning and meeting new cultures. An open, benevolent approach enables them to embrace strangers as old friends, and they are genuinely interested in the belief patterns that make people act and live in

certain ways. Sagittarian energy is restless, explorative, optimistic, always seeking to understand – but in a different way than Virgo or Gemini, two other mutable signs who seek detail and category. Sagittarius takes the fiery theme of Aries and Leo and projects it out into the world through its search for the larger pattern underlying social behaviour. A major theme for Sagittarius is the search for meaning, and whether or not this expresses through superficial or serious avenues, it keeps Sagittarius active and enthusiastically seeking all his life. A dilemma that comes from this search for meaning is the struggle with certainty: discovering universal laws gives them confidence that justice is possible, but the truth that informs the different moral systems of the world is inevitably infinite and beyond classification. Independent, proud, boisterous, the Sagittarian type needs plenty of space for experimentation and play, both in matters of career and of the heart. Although they will rebel against stuffy society and meaningless rules, there is an innate respect for strong individuals whose spiritual integrity and honesty shines out. This respect for integrity informs their behaviour – allegiance is an expression of love for Sagittarius. They are not good at pretending. Sagittarian energy is warm, friendly, alert, helpful, but can also be bombastic, careless and flighty. Their love for the large and dramatic means they can be sloppy and depend on generalizations and argumentation. So huge is the sense of potential they carry within, they can drastically over-promise and over-extend with too many irons in the fire. When they meet their mortal limits, their arrows come down to earth and depression may take over whilst they learn to adapt to the demands of the world. Their resilience and faith in life's bounty usually wins in the end. Planets in Sagittarius will express their energies in an open, warm and spontaneous way. If Sagittarius is strongly emphasized in your chart, your life may be dominated by some kind of quest for meaning

which impels you to reach far beyond the boundaries of normal existence. The Sagittarian author and satirist Mark Twain expressed this sign's restless, ironic mind and irrepressible spirit in his work, and about truth he wrote:

> Why shouldn't truth be stranger than fiction? Fiction, after all, has to make sense.

Sagittarius rules the thighs and its motto is 'I aspire'.

♑

CAPRICORN

THE SUN PASSES THROUGH CAPRICORN BETWEEN ABOUT 22 DECEMBER–19 JANUARY.

Capricorn is a negative Cardinal Earth sign which marks the winter solstice and the beginning of the slow increase of sunlight. In the northern hemisphere this is the point of most limited light, when activity within the natural world is still, the life force having withdrawn to prepare silently, within the tomb of the earth, for rebirth at spring. Capricorn's symbol is the fish-goat, indicating the ancient origins of this most ambitious and determined of the Earth signs. Another mythical goat figure is that of the Greek god Pan who stood for the wild fertility of nature. The mountain goat is more commonly associated with Capricorn, representing this sign's upwardly-mobile aspirations, as well as the giddy goat's more sensual nature. Capricorn's ruling planet is Saturn, the god of structure, authority, responsibility and tradition. Saturn also represents the 'golden age', a mythical time of perfect order, when spiritual purpose is married with material form to produce the highest possible objective world order. The Capricornian personality is hardworking, cautious, serious and reserved, intent on understanding and constructively applying the wisdom of the past in order to build a secure future. Wanting to build things that last, Capricorn is not easily discouraged by difficult challenges. This is an individual with definite aims, someone who is not interested in 'easy' tasks or empty praise. Success may be measured by material security and position, but Capricorn places even greater importance on having endured a long, testing commitment which proves his or her stamina and ability. Such serious staying power often makes it hard for Capricorn to relax and enjoy life. They want to be occupied with purposeful activities and difficult challenges which are grist to their mill. Early in life the Capricorn individual seems filled with adult concerns and will often take on responsibilities within the family which weigh heavily on the soul. But it is practical experience which teaches them and gives them the confidence they crave. Dependable and loyal, Capricorns keep their promises and make excellent leaders. However, the weak Capricorn, driven by a powerful need for recognition, can slip into the 'end-justifies-the-means' syndrome before realizing that his or her empire has been built on faulty foundations. Failure of any kind is hard to bear, for their inner critic tends to be more exacting than any external authority figure they have known. Saturn's rulership emphasizes this sign's concern with order, duty and discipline. Preferring to hide their vulnerability, Capricorns often endure periods of real gloom and struggle on their own. As they get older and more secure in their capabilities, Capricorn paradoxically grows younger and more playful. Because their maturity and wisdom comes from years of hard experience, their advice is valued highly. Planets in Capricorn will express their energies in a controlled, efficient, prudent way. If Capricorn is strongly emphasized in your chart, you will spend a great deal of your life defining and pursuing professional ambitions of which you can be proud. Stephen Hawking's life is testimony to the hardy Capricorn spirit: he overcame great physical obstacles to pursue his pioneering work in astronomy. He wrote:

> The progress of the human race in understanding the universe has established a small corner of order in an increasingly disordered universe.

Capricorn rules the bones and skeletal system, and its motto is 'I order'.

AQUARIUS

THE SUN PASSES THROUGH AQUARIUS BETWEEN
ABOUT 20 JANUARY–18 FEBRUARY.

Aquarius is the positive Fixed Air sign that brings the yearly phase when we behold a vast, still world in the depths of winter. The symbol for Aquarius is the Water-bearer, the urn of the flowing waters of life. In both Sumerian and Egyptian mythologies, great sky goddesses poured forth the healing waters. The symbol for the Egyptian goddess Nut was a round vase, and in the Celtic tradition the Aquarian urn is linked with the cauldron of the goddess Cerridwen, which bestowed the gift of prophecy. But Aquarius is an Air sign whose nourishing draught is truth itself as embodied in universal ideals. This sign takes a broad, humanitarian view of what society could be. Aquarius is ruled by both Saturn and Uranus. Its Saturnian influence gives Aquarius its value of principles and the laws of thought; its Uranian side is both futuristic and individualistic, for Aquarius wants to ensure that those same laws, supporting the framework of society, protect the rights and dignity of each individual. As a personality, Aquarius is intellectual, unconventional, visionary, often scientific, independent and usually altruistic. These individuals have an anarchic streak and are interested in leaderless, egalitarian communities. Friendship is their matrix – friendship and truth – and they are drawn to new people with an openness and curiosity that is both liberating and at times exasperating. This is because so often Aquarius is not aware of their own emotional need, nor of the more subtle nuances of emotional relationships. Although friendly, gregarious and progressive, Aquarius can become rigid and doctrinaire in their beliefs due to their unshakeable faith in ideals. A certain naivety and benign eccentricity makes the Aquarian individual a natural catalyst in groups, for they challenge assumptions and wake people up. The Aquarian monk Thomas Merton, who challenged the traditional Trappist way of living, was described as 'a question demanding an answer'. Aquarian idealism is not always easy to live with, and ironically they are often loners, more at home with their ideas and principles than their feelings. Although Aquarians are independent people who need a lot of space for self-expression, they are not without passion. It's just that they find it easier to express this in politics or collective movements than in one-to-one relationships. Planets in Aquarius will express their energies in a dispassionate, thoughtful, independent way. If Aquarius is strongly emphasized in your chart, you will seek a truthful, meaningful role in a social group, and you may need to risk being the outsider, or challenging the status quo, in order to contribute to the greater good. Thomas Merton wrote many books, and in his monastic and wider collective life embodied the Aquarian idea, which is expressed beautifully in his words:

> I am the incarnation of everybody and the zones of reassurance
> … I live in the social cages of joy.

Aquarius rules the lower legs and the circulation, and its motto is 'I reform'.

PISCES

THE SUN PASSES THROUGH PISCES BETWEEN
ABOUT 19 FEBRUARY–20 MARCH.

Pisces is a negative Mutable Water sign which brings us to the phase just preceding the advent of spring. In the northern hemisphere, daylight is increasing and the stirrings of new life can be felt, bringing an anticipation of renewal. Just as we long to celebrate life vanquishing the darkness of winter (as we do in the ancient ritual we know as Easter), Pisces has a longing for eternity, where it can merge with life in the oceanic depths. The symbol for Pisces is the two fishes, each swimming in a different direction, symbolizing the conflictual urges of man's instincts versus his immortal spirit. Neptune, the god of the sea, is the ruler of this sign, suggesting that the depths of the collective unconscious hold the buried treasure of Pisces' imagination. Pisces grapples with the duality of human nature – its darkness and its light, its transience and its lasting beauty. Pisces contains many contradictions and possibilities which enable it to identify with the entire spectrum of human experience: the saint, the sage, the siren, the sinner. Jesus was known as 'the fisher of men' whose love and compassion gave him the power to sacrifice his earthly life for all humanity. Many Pisceans have a similar self-sacrificing, forgiving, compassionate nature and are capable of emotionally identifying with the plight of the suffering. But they can also sacrifice their fondest dreams due to vacillation and lack of confidence. Although there is a sensual, sociable, happy-go-lucky side to this sign, Piscean individuals usually protect a very private part of their soul which needs to commune with their dreams and fantasies. This side of Pisces dislikes exactitude; defining themselves in too literal a way feels deadening, and as a result they can suddenly drift away and sometimes miss opportunities through aimlessness. Because Pisces is the last sign, its ego impulses often veer towards disengagement with life: all the different options and roles in life seem equally valid. This turning away from self-expression can take a more despairing route, such as in alcoholism or drug addiction. Or conversely, Pisces may seek to relieve a similar despair in others through service in the healing professions. This sign is very receptive to the emotional currents in others, is intuitive, psychic, and seeks to communicate its perceptions to the world. Theatre offers an ideal platform for Pisces; here Pisces can move in and out of different identities with ease. Planets in Pisces will express their energies in a diffuse and sensitive way. If Pisces is strongly emphasized in your chart, you will need to find a creative voice to express your experience of the beauty, pain and duality of life. The psychic Arthur Guirdham, with both Sun and Moon in Pisces, expressed a uniquely Piscean perspective when he said:

Joy is the voice of the escaped psyche.

Pisces rules the feet, and its motto is 'I redeem'.

THE CORNERS OF THE SOUL
– THE HOUSES OF THE HOROSCOPE

In every corner of my soul, there is an altar to a different god.

FERNANDO PESSOA

J ust as there are 12 signs, there are 12 astrological houses that closely reflect the meanings of the signs. Although this book does not attempt to deal with the complex astronomical realities of astrology, it is important to understand that in astrology we deal with two kinds of movement – the movement of the Earth and the other celestial bodies around the Sun, and the movement of the Earth on its axis during a 24-hour period. The zodiacal signs are subdivisions of the first kind of movement – that is, of the Earth's yearly journey around the Sun – and the houses are subdivisions of the second – that is, of the Earth's rotation in a day, from the sun's rising at dawn, to its culmination at noon, to its setting at dusk, to midnight in the depths of night and back again to dawn. All the planets likewise rise, culminate and set every day.

THE ANGLES: ASCENDANT AND MID-HEAVEN AND THEIR OPPOSITE POINTS

Astrologers use very specific mathematical calculations in order to 'cast' the horoscope or birth chart for a specific time and place of birth. This is why astrologers want to know the exact time of birth, for this is what brings the zodiac down to earth for each individual. The moment of birth determines the degree of the zodiac rising over the Eastern horizon – the 'sunrise' point – also called the Ascendant. This point describes the unique personality which is coming into being. The Ascendant represents the individual view of the world, and the way in which the complexities of the whole chart will relate to the environment. The inner world meets the outer world here, and from this juxtaposition our sense of identity emerges: our physical appearance, our typical style of response, our overall orientation and unique mind-set. The Ascendant is the beginning point of the first house, the house of the self.

In this book we do not attempt to teach calculation of the birth chart. For readers who want to learn this, there are many books which provide step-by-step instruction, such as *The Complete Astrologer* by Julia and Derek Parker and *The Practical Astrologer* by Nick Campion. If you are on the internet, the simplest and quickest way to calculate your Ascendant and birth chart is to visit the Swiss Astrodienst site at <u>www.astro.ch</u> which has a free on-line chart calculation service. The enormous advantage of this site is that it includes the very latest information about time changes, summer time and the latitude and longitude of over 200,000 cities, towns and villages around the world. For further details, see the section on Astrological Resources.

THE ASCENDANT: ENTERING THE WORLD

The Ascendant or Rising Sign is so important that it bears further definition. The psychologist Carl Jung wrote about the 'persona', or the outer mask we wear in the world in order to function in an ordinary, everyday sort of way. There is nothing intrinsically false about this mask, for we all need a protective lens through which we perceive the world and allow others to perceive us. The Ascendant therefore has a socially adaptive function as well as a self-introductory function: we present ourselves to the world in a certain way, but there is always much more beneath the surface. When we feel close and safe with people, we reveal more of ourselves, more of our chart – the inner complexities of our nature.

For example, at a social gathering, the person with Sagittarius rising will breeze into the room as though he already knows everyone, and his casual, open, if somewhat clumsy style helps to break the ice. He exudes an enviable optimism and friendliness which, if you get to know him intimately, takes on a far more sober demeanour when he lets you see his serious Capricorn Moon. The person with Pisces rising could be on her third drink already and compassionately engaged in conversation with the person whose leg is in a cast. All the while her Mercury conjunct Pluto is gathering new material for her next novel. The Leo Ascendant arrives late, carrying three bottles of expensive champagne: heads turn, for his warmth and radiance is irresistible. But actually, he feels most comfortable in the kitchen where his Sun–Venus conjunction in Cancer goes to work preparing the sumptuous baked Alaska he's promised. Gemini rising is chatting with everyone, but her Scorpio Sun is not letting on about what she really feels. Not yet, and maybe never. All of these caricatured personality types have many other layers to their natures, but it is the Ascendant which is first perceived, which leads our way into the world. But the

Ascendant is even more than this. Its qualities denote the individual path that will lead to self-realization. As astrologer Liz Greene has described it, the Sun is the kind of hero we are, but the Ascendant is the journey that takes us on the hero's quest.

THE DESCENDANT

Opposite this rising degree is the Descendant, which describes the 'other', the natural partner. The Descendant marks the cusp of the seventh house, the realm of our experience of other people: what we want from them, give to them, get from them, and project onto them. Planets in this house will have a major influence on the way we interact with others – what we have to learn, to confront and to enjoy. The Ascendant and Descendant form an axis, a polarity: neither can be fully understood without the other, suggesting that our own identity is intimately influenced by our relationship with others.

THE MIDHEAVEN: WHAT WILL I BE WHEN I GROW UP?

The moment of birth also gives the Midheaven. This is the uppermost point of the chart, symbolizing the height of worldly success and public position. The Midheaven or 'MC' (Medium Coeli or 'middle of the sky') represents our aspirations and ambitions, and describes the type of career we will seek to develop. It represents status and self-esteem, and the image we want to cultivate in the world, the way we would like to be seen. Whereas we express the qualities of the Ascendant naturally and spontaneously, without self-consciousness or effort, we consciously aspire to develop and express the qualities of the Midheaven. The MC also describes our experience of authority figures, and the ideals which govern our interactions with the world. In one of Freud's outstanding papers, 'The Ego and the Id' (1923), he describes the development of the internal

agent of judgement in a way that succinctly expresses the dynamics of the Midheaven and its opposite point, the IC (Imum Coeli or 'bottom of the sky'), which together form the 'parental' axis:

> … here we have that higher nature, in this ego ideal or super-ego, the representative of our relation to our parents. When we were little children we knew these higher natures, we admired them and feared them; and later we took them into ourselves … What has belonged to the lowest part of the mental life of each of us is changed, through the formation of the ideal, into what is highest in the human mind by our scale of values.

What does it feel like to be helpless and dependent on authority figures? And how does it feel to be an authority figure, taking responsibility for ourselves and others? The MC describes this dynamic, and also the qualities we wish to develop and work for in the outer world.

IMUM COELI

The opposite point of the Midheaven is the lowest point of the chart, called the Imum Coeli or 'IC'. Just as the MC denotes our outermost role in the world, the IC describes the innermost and the least exposed area of experience: early home life, ancestral influence, and the unconscious roots of personality. This point links us to our personal past, the ancestral soil, and therefore indicates our need for privacy and security and the way we feel about home and family life. In the Placidus House system, the IC is the beginning point of the fourth house. The IC and MC form an axis of innermost and outermost life experience.

The Ascendant, Descendant, Midheaven and Immum Coeli are called the four angles of a chart. Planets which are conjoined at these points have marked importance and power in an individual's personality, and are referred to as 'angular' planets.

The Ascendant–Descendant line divides the circle into upper and lower halves, the lower part symbolizing a more subjective experience or consciousness, and the upper part symbolizing objective consciousness and experience in the outer world. The Midheaven–Imum Coeli line divides the circle into an Eastern and Western hemisphere; the Eastern hemisphere is to do with the self and self-activity, whilst the Western hemisphere is linked with others' influence and the way this impacts on an individual's life. A chart with an emphasis of planets located in the lower half of the Ascendant–Descendant axis, for example, suggests a more self-oriented, interior, personal bias whilst an emphasis of planets in the upper half suggests much activity in the outer world.

These four quadrants of the chart are further trisected to finally give the 12 houses or domains, places of life experience and psychological development. Although there are different house systems that result in slightly different intermediate house cusps, there is universal agreement among astrologers on the meaning of the houses, the foundations of which stretch back into antiquity.

The word 'house' suggests a place where one resides, and this is exactly what occurs in a birth chart: the planets occupy different sectors or compartments of the chart, showing the area where their energies will 'be at home' and function automatically. And although it may be a crude analogy, people have different 'compartments' to their personalities. Some of these compartments are very visible and accessible, just like the first and tenth houses, whereas others are more hidden and private, as are the fourth and eighth houses.

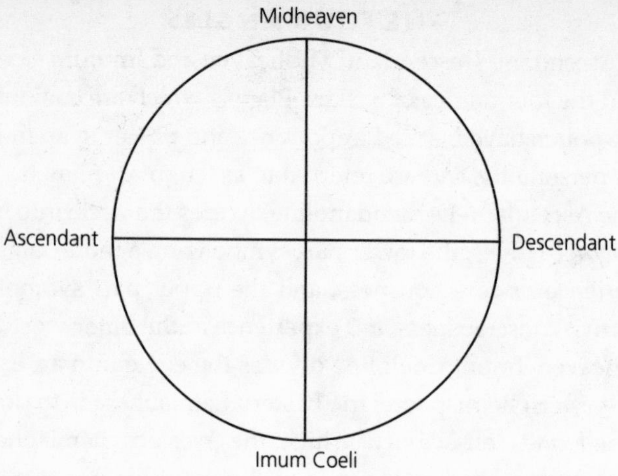

Figure 7.1. The Four Angles

The houses of the birth chart are numbered in sequence from the first to the twelfth house in a reverse direction from the diurnal motion of the planets, beginning at the Ascendant. The meanings of the houses have a close affinity with the twelve signs, e.g. Aries as the first sign places great value on self-motivation and potency, and the first house is the house of all things to do with the self meeting the outside world.

FIRST HOUSE

The race advances only by the extra achievements of the individual. You are the individual.

CHARLES TOWNE

This is the house of the 'self' – self-awareness, self-image, self-activity, perceiving the world from a unique subjective standpoint. It relates to the outer persona, body type and personal style, where we meet others face to face and make a first

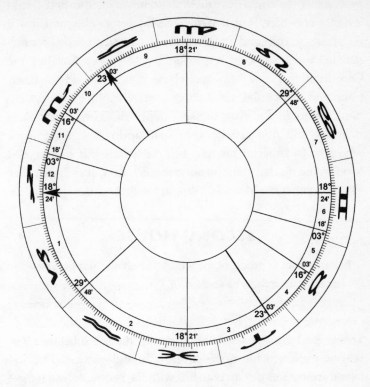

Figure 7.2. The Twelve Houses

impression. The Ascendant begins the first house, and one's personal interests and approach to life are defined by this 'rising sign'. The individual is 'earthed' at birth in this specific point, which signifies the manner and direction in which he or she will express the combined qualities of the whole chart. Signs and planets in this house brand or colour the personality very powerfully, and are expressed in an innocently assertive way – directly, physically, spontaneously, openly. For example, if Mercury is in this house, the individual's quick, nervous, enquiring attitude will be a dominant and very visible component of the personality. Saturn with the Ascendant or in the first house inhibits, constricts, but also deepens the personality which will be strongly coloured by a serious mental attitude, conservatism, and a sense of responsibility. Margaret Thatcher, the Conservative Prime Minister whose policies called for discipline and self-denial, has Saturn exactly conjunct the Ascendant. Pluto in the first house colours the personality with intensity and mystery. Leonardo DiCaprio, the young actor who rose to fame for his role as a passionate but star-crossed lover in the modern film *Romeo and Juliet*, as well as *Titanic*, has Pluto conjunct the Moon in Libra in the first house.

SECOND HOUSE

> If a rich man is proud of his wealth, he should not be praised until it is known how he employs it.
>
> SOCRATES

This is the house of personal resources, the life substance that will be exploited for survival, growth, and success. The first house announces our arrival, but with the second house we get 'stuck in' to life and find out what we are made of. We experience our second house by feeling effective in the world and through enjoying the physical world around us. We feel pride in our capacity to earn our own living; it makes us feel 'real'. Signs and planets in this sector indicate how we develop and build an identity, what we value and feel we must hold on to, what we work with to 'ground' ourselves in life, and the specific innate talents we possess which may attract wealth and which we use to build secure foundations for living. In general, the second house shows our attitudes towards the material world and possessions. For example, a person with Venus in the second house values beauty, love and the good things of the earth; she could be adept at creating a beautiful working environment and may attract wealth due to her positive feeling about the material world (although aspects from other planets would enhance or limit this). Moon in the second house values emotional security, attaches long-lasting emotional significance to possessions, and could earn money through serving or caring for others. Princess Diana had the Moon in the second house, and it could be said that her greatest resource was her 'personal touch' in her approach to empathizing with others and caring for those in need.

THIRD HOUSE

> Good communication is as stimulating as black coffee, and just as
> hard to sleep after.
>
> ANNE MORROW LINDBERGH

This is the house of mental functioning – thinking, learning and communicating; the intellect exploring the world, ideas and relationships. This is where we interact with others in our family and home, and in school and the wider community. Developmentally, this sphere corresponds to the stage of learning to walk and acquiring language, and how we employ both acquisitions to explore our environment. In the second house we gain security; in the third we gain mobility. Signs and planets in this house say something about our experience with siblings; they also express our approach to learning and the exchange of information. For example, a person with Neptune in the third house would have a highly imaginative and intuitive approach to learning and communication, and may even discover they can write poetry (and communicate telepathically!), but they also might have a propensity to day-dream and to wander and easily get lost in their environment. With Mars in the third

house, the mind is forceful, eager, maybe highly strung and prone to get into verbal slinging matches (especially with siblings). This person knows that 'thoughts are things'; for him, getting his message across is an act of will. Oprah Winfrey, the hugely successful talk show hostess who fires questions and gets the knowledge she wants, has Mars in the third house.

FOURTH HOUSE

The family is the nucleus of civilization.

WILL DURANT

This is the house of early home origins. It is often referred to as the 'midnight' part of the chart, referring to that which is most habitual and unconscious. This house reveals our past, our family roots and traditions, the emotional soil in which our identity learned to grow, and therefore the stuff we are made of. Signs and planets in this sector reveal something about our experience of belonging to a first 'group' or clan, as well as describing the way we experienced our mother or caretaker. Parental influence is shown as well as how it feels to be in a hierarchical relationship. The realm of our earliest experiences becomes our psychological future; this house describes those earliest experiences and how they were digested to become deeply imbedded patterns that are passed on to subsequent generations. This house also reveals how we retreat into our own private domestic world, how we like our home to be. Mercury in the fourth house suggests an early life that had a distinctly intellectual feel, or one in which there was lots of discussion, communication, movement and travel, and constant to-ing and fro-ing and busy learning. The Sun in the fourth house is an individual who identifies strongly with their roots, who seeks to dominate their own private world, and who will

seek to make inherited values conscious and individual. The American actress Sissy Spacek has the Sun in the fourth house; when working on a film she moves her whole family – children, grandparents, pets and all – to be there with her.

FIFTH HOUSE

No matter how old you get, if you can keep the desire to be creative, you're keeping the man-child alive.

JOHN CASSAVETES

This is the realm of pleasure and where what we do is for our own enjoyment. In this house we take one step away from the fourth and discover our unique talents and the delight of being creative, of nurturing and engaging with that which springs from within us. It is here that we indulge in self-expression for our own pleasure. This is the house of playing, loving, risking, children and all the creative 'products' of the self. It therefore embraces a wide area – love affairs, speculation and creative activity in general. Signs and planets in this house give an indication as to our enjoyment of the creative experience and the way in which we achieve the feeling of being unique, important, 'someone special' who is appreciated and valued for simply being us. It is intimately linked with the experience of being a child, when we play in imaginal realms and believe the sun shines for us alone. With Saturn in the fifth house, there can be difficulty in freely expressing one's creativity. Saturn brings fears that one's creative efforts will be found wanting, but on the other hand, Saturn here gives enormous commitment to work seriously on creative projects. Venus in the fifth house enjoys beauty and romance and can indulge with great style in pleasurable activities. Barbara Cartland, the author of many romantic novels, has Venus in the fifth house. Also with this

position was Princess Diana who was admired for, among other things, her colourful fashion sense and the way she brought dynamic, flirtatious, Venusian energy into any environment.

SIXTH HOUSE

When people are serving, life is no longer meaningless.

JOHN GARDNER

This is the province of the chores and routines which keep our normal everyday life ticking over. It is here that we establish those habit patterns (shopping, eating, brushing our teeth, sleeping) which keep us grounded in our bodies. Therefore, this is the sector of the chart linked with health and the mind–body connection: when we look after our bodies, we feel, think, and function optimally; we can be more creative. It is also the house of work and service, where we dedicate ourselves through practice to developing the talents we discovered in the fifth house. 'Practice makes perfect' is one of the mottoes of this house, reflecting the fact that becoming an accomplished artist or craftsman in any field requires constant vigilance and effort. Elbert Hubbard once said 'we work to become, not to acquire', suggesting that the work we do in life is what we need in order to become who we are. Through constant adjustment and attending to what needs doing, we get there in the end. This house reflects our attitudes to employment, to being an employee and also to employing others. Signs and planets in this sector show how we bring different aspects of our nature – mind, body, feelings – into an integral and happily working 'whole'. Jupiter in the sixth can create extremes in health regimes, and work could involve travel, education or sports. Moon in the sixth finds security and comfort by clocking into the daily routine and seeing to the practical needs of others. Adelle Davis, the American nutritionist who wrote *Let's Eat Right to Keep Fit*, had Moon conjunct Pluto in the sixth in Gemini.

SEVENTH HOUSE

Take away love and our earth is a tomb.

ROBERT BROWNING

'No man is an island' is the message of the seventh house. It is here at the opposite point to the Ascendant/first house that we make our debut into the outer world – there are people out there we need to meet. This is the house of relationships – how we meet 'the other' in life, the kind of person that complements our nature and whom we are attracted to. Its qualities reflect the marriage partner and also, interestingly, 'open enemies' – those with whom we provoke direct opposition or conflict, such as opponents in legal matters, as opposed to the 'hidden enemies' of the twelfth house. This house will show what we easily 'project' onto others and, through close encounters with the other, can learn to balance and reintegrate within ourselves. Through important relationships we find out about qualities in ourselves that are unconscious. In the realm of the seventh, we become aware of our need for love and relationship, and yet, how much do we co-operate, and how much can we assert ourselves? Grappling with these issues and balancing needs in relationships is part of the task of the seventh house. Signs and planets in this house describe the qualities we seek and experience through egalitarian relationships. Uranus in the seventh seeks freedom-loving qualities in a relationship, and sometimes finds it hard to make a commitment. Jupiter in the seventh will grow and feel good in the presence of others, and may seek understanding, wealth and prestige

PRINCIPLES OF ASTROLOGY

through the partner. Jacqueline Kennedy Onassis, whose two marriages brought her both status and enormous wealth, had Jupiter in the seventh.

EIGHTH HOUSE

If it is not erotic, it is not interesting.

FERNANDO ARRABAL

This house takes the seventh house one stage further: here we meet our deepest need for intimacy and our feelings about dependence. The eighth house governs our attitudes towards passionate intimacy and raw, instinctual experience, and the sharing of material resources. What happens when two people attempt to 'merge', when we dive into another individual's world with our own values, hopes and dreads? We meet at the deepest level, expose parts of our nature that we normally keep hidden, and experience a transcendence of our finite self through sexual ecstasy. This is the house of sex and shared possessions, of psychological change and regeneration, of death and rebirth, and of combining energies with an intimate 'other' for a mutual enhancement of power. Eighth house transactions can be a catalyst for fears about survival which are rooted in early childhood trauma; power struggles can then ensue which can lead to the divorce court, unless we use these experiences for greater self-knowledge and self-healing. This house governs the biological transitions of life: birth, puberty, sexual potency and death. Signs and planets in this house say something about our physical appetites – do we control them or go with them? A person with the Sun in the eighth house would find her life path through deep and courageous involvement with others. Coretta Scott King, the widow of Martin Luther King Jr., has Sun in the eighth; she survived many personal attacks throughout the civil rights movement, and continued her husband's work after his assassination. Freud had Saturn in the eighth, which is fitting for a man who spent his professional life studying the links between mental health, infant sexuality and the death instinct.

NINTH HOUSE

Neither man nor nation can exist without a sublime idea.

DOSTOEVSKI

After the cathartic experiences of the eighth house, we surface in the ninth house to gain a greater perspective on our journey through life. This is the house of the 'higher mind' – education, philosophy, religion. Its province includes our need for enduring precepts by which we 'make meaning' and navigate through life's unfolding process. This sector of the chart reveals the way we seek underlying patterns in life, the way we make sense of what happens to us, the way we fit things into a larger whole. It also describes our experience of travel and new cultural experiences: do we welcome or fear mind-expanding experiences? The way we approach education and the development of our intellect is shown by this house. Signs and planets in this sector say something about our larger mind-set and the perspective through which we learn the rules of the game of life. If Saturn is here, we take a scientific approach and prefer the conventional road to knowledge, a more left-brain emphasis; but we may easily feel insecure and daunted by what we don't know and understand with absolute certitude. Mars in the ninth suggests a forceful, 'positive-thinking' approach to philosophy and belief systems. If Neptune is here there is a more intuitive, all-inclusive, artistic and heart-oriented approach to understanding the world. The great mythologist

Joseph Campbell had Neptune in the ninth; he taught and wrote about the unifying vitality of the great transcultural myths whose meaning transcends words. Albert Einstein had Jupiter in the ninth; although he was a scientist, he was also a philosopher who felt deep moral concern regarding the power his discoveries unleashed on the world.

TENTH HOUSE

Every individual has a place to fill in the world and is important in some respect, whether he chooses to be so or not.

NATHANIEL HAWTHORNE

This is the house of vocational aspirations and career, of one's role in public life, as well as representing parental influence in the shaping of the individual personality in the world. The tenth house incorporates the MC or Midheaven whose qualities reflect the way we would like to be seen and appreciated by others, the characteristics and ideals we espouse and for which we want to be respected. This is the highest point of the chart and represents the ultimate flowering of one's role and status in society, and the esteem we receive for our influence in the world. The zodiacal journey reaches a pinnacle here: from being a 'somebody' in potential, we arrive here at the tenth house to be a 'somebody' in objective reality. How do we feel about authority figures, and how do we feel when we are in positions of authority? The tenth house addresses these questions. Signs and planets in this house reveal something about our ambitions, the way we carry responsibility, and our aims to achieve recognition. Those with Uranus in the tenth could follow a revolutionary path to career success, and may gain recognition for changing or challenging the status quo. Vanessa Redgrave, the accomplished and rebellious actress who is also a vociferous political activist, has Uranus conjunct the MC. Pluto in the tenth suggests a career involving research into the hidden and healing power of the mind (psychology, psychiatry), or other forms of the use, or abuse, of power (politics, espionage, the occult). But equally those with Pluto in the tenth may feel impotent in the face of all the power they project out into the world. The famous crime fiction writer Agatha Christie had Pluto in the tenth house.

ELEVENTH HOUSE

Love thy neighbor as thyself, but choose your neighborhood.

LOUISE BEAL

This is the house of ideals, social values and friendship. It rules the 'collectives' and groups one identifies with in order to feel connected to something larger than oneself. We are linked to friends and associates by the underlying ideals we cherish and wish to see expressed in society. Its opposite house, the fifth, is where we discover our unique self with our very own talents; but it is here in the realm of larger groups of people that we put our talents to work in the service of a collective purpose: the individual engaged with the collective. In this sector of life we participate in a 'group consciousness' and experience a sense of belonging in a different way than we do in the fourth house. The eleventh house is where we gain a sense of identity with a group – social, professional, political, religious – and that affiliation will augment, dissipate or repress our individual identity depending on planetary configurations in that house. Signs and planets in this sector reveal the way we relate to the 'group-mind', the way we fit into the society in which we live. Saturn in the eleventh house searches for a more secure sense of belonging through professional groups. Uranus in the eleventh

house may play the 'wild card in the deck' and gravitate towards groups that work for the liberation of humanity in some way. The actress-turned-politician Glenda Jackson, who is known for her convictions about contributing to the collective good, has Venus conjunct Uranus in the eleventh house. In the chart of Prince Charles, Uranus is in the eleventh house; he is known for his alternative views, a fact which has brought a new, challenging influence into his 'group', the monarchy.

TWELFTH HOUSE

In solitude, be a multitude to thyself.

TIBULLUS

We begin with the first house and the urge to manifest the 'self' as real and distinct from others; and we end with the twelfth house where the urge is to identify with something larger than ourselves, with the universal matrix of all life. This is the house of endings, sometimes referred to as the house of self-undoing, for it represents the yearning for liberation from earthly confines. Here the urge is to withdraw from egocentric struggles for worldly attainment, to cultivate the joys of solitude, to commune with our innermost self which we intuit can only be communed with, rather than defined with certitude. It is also linked with 'hidden enemies', or those aspects of life and of our own natures which we block out and which end up sabotaging us at the last moment. Sometimes we relinquish more than we bargain for: we may try to escape life's struggles by becoming behind-the-scene workers and helpers, the extreme of which is the martyr who takes on the sufferings of others. Signs and planets in this house indicate what one sacrifices for the larger good of others, or how one approaches solitude and working 'behind the scenes'. Planets here also express their energies in strategic and unconscious ways – they never want to be 'seen'. Mars in the twelfth is motivated for the common good rather than merely for personal gain, but may sometimes miss personal opportunities due to his reluctance to separate out his own desires from the collective. Venus in the twelfth communes with beauty on her own, and sometimes indulges in clandestine romances. Camilla Parker-Bowles has the Sun, Moon and Venus in the twelfth, a fitting placement for someone who is famous for her 'behind-the-scenes' romance.

PUTTING IT ALL TOGETHER

The beginning holds the seed of all that is to follow.

I CHING: 30

One always hopes to become someone only to find out in the end that one is several.

RAYMOND DEVOS

I n this chapter we show how astrologers put together the richly varied cast of characters in the average birth chart in order to present a coherent but multi-dimensional picture of a whole human being. It should be emphasized that an astrologer's analysis of a chart is not a definitive statement, but rather an exploration of a multi-faceted image. In practice, this exploration is a two-way process involving the astrologer and the client; the astrologer's understanding is presented and also 'checked out' with the client, which elicits participation and collaboration, and an invitation for the client to explore the symbolism of the chart alongside the astrologer.

In fact, when learning how to understand a birth chart, the best and most relevant information comes from its owner. For example, if you have a chart in front of you with Moon opposed Uranus, you start with the principles: Moon = feeling, imagination, belonging, safety; and Uranus = sudden change, freedom, originality. Together the two principles could mean many things, such as (1) a highly original imagination, (2) a person whose mother was unusual, (3) a freedom-loving personality, (4) a dislike of emotional commitment. So what does it mean for *this* person? Here is where describing the principles and then eliciting feedback from the owner of the chart will teach you astrology! And the best way to learn is to practise with friends and family. If you decide to study astrology for yourself, then it can become a personal tool and a solo exploration – you and the symbols.

Sometimes a person will come seeking apparently straight-forward 'advice' about money or career issues, but a competent astrologer will study and refer to the whole chart, for there is no compartment of an individual's life which is separate from the whole life pattern. It must be emphasized that all inter-pretative work should be entered into with the utmost care and responsibility, for people can be needlessly frightened, and even harmed, by careless or negative statements. Astrolog-ical interpretation should be an exploration, an 'opening up' process, and a catalyst to greater self-understanding. Insights that come from chart analysis can help to unlock thorny per-sonal issues, and the beginner in astrology should always remember that seemingly 'difficult' aspects give depth, endur-ance and positive potential to character.

LOGIC AND INTUITION

It should also be emphasized that an astrologer uses intuition as much as intellect in the exploration of a birth chart. After carefully setting up the chart and studying its structure and its features one by one and the way they all inter-relate, the astrologer will pause in order to allow *intuitive imagination* to go to work. The facts have been carefully assembled, but then the astrologer must simply come back to the chart and see or apprehend it as one would a painting or a mandala. One must simply and respectfully *behold* the integrity of the image: it is unique, a map of an individual psyche, a soul's contract with time and space, a complete theatrical work with its inherent tensions and meaningful trajectory. This act of 'imaginatively apprehending without reason' often yields valuable images of how particular dynamics in the chart may express themselves. In a subtle way, this leads the consultation in a fertile direction. Left-brain and right-brain activity operate hand-in-hand in an astrologer's work, as they do in any truly creative science-art.

AN ANALYSIS OF THE BIRTH CHART OF PRINCESS DIANA

Perhaps no other individual has captured the imagination of the collective psyche in recent years as powerfully as the late Princess of Wales. For this reason, we will use her chart for the purposes of this chapter. What would an astrologer say about her birth chart? What were the themes and sub-personalities in her life drama? What insights would be emphasized about her strengths and weaknesses, her potential for happy or difficult relationships, career ambitions and personal development? It is important to remember that interpretation depends a lot on the context of a person's life. Many people were born on the same day and moment as Princess Diana, but only she became a future queen of England. However, regardless of personal context, the astrological principles will still be the same in essence, and will express in accord with their natures.

Whilst all the features of the chart are important and the chart needs to be appreciated as a whole, most astrologers will, as a lead into the interpretation, first consider the position of the Sun, the Moon, and the Ascendant.

Sun in
Cancer
(Cardinal
Water

Emotionally attuned, sensitive, maternal, clannish, imaginative, fluctuating moods but deeply loyal, need for intimacy and belonging, tenacious, centres identity through others, a need to share, to be mirrored.

As a Sun Cancerian, Princess Diana's life was centred in the dimension of feeling, family and belonging. Her Sun in Cancer tells us that emotional security was vital to her wellbeing as well as being something which she herself could create and give to others. Her essential nature, like the nature of water itself, was fluid and ever-changing, and therefore she was happiest when her fluidity was being contained and channelled by someone strong and solid. Emotional relationships were of paramount importance to the Princess, and her emotional concerns revolved around those who were 'her own', those who were part of her intimate clan. True to her Cancerian nature, she had worked as a nursery school teacher and was most confident in her role as a mother. With her sons William and Harry, Diana could really be herself: she felt needed, could be warm, playful, loving, nurturing, in tune with the needs of the young and vulnerable. Timidity and impressionability plagued Diana always, but as her identity evolved through the feminine roles of royal consort and mother, she began to enjoy the publicity she attracted. Recognition for her Cancerian qualities – tenderness, loyalty, practicality, responding to needs – gave her self-esteem. Typically, her

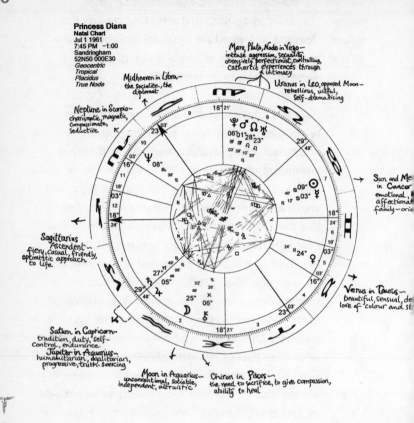

Princess Diana
Natal Chart
Jul 1 1961
7:45 PM −1:00
Sandringham
52N50 000E30
Geocentric
Tropical
Placidus
True Node

Mars, Pluto, Node in Virgo—
intense aggression, sexuality,
obsessively perfectionist, controlling,
Cathartic experiences through
intimacy

Midheaven in Libra—
the Socialite, the
diplomat

Uranus in Leo, opposed Moon—
rebellious, wilful,
self-dramatising

Neptune in Scorpio—
charismatic, magnetic,
compassionate,
seductive.

Sun and Me
in Cancer
emotional,
affectional
family-orie

Sagittarius
Ascendent—
fiery, casual, friendly,
optimistic approach
to life

Venus in Taurus—
beautiful, sensual, de
love of colour and st

Saturn in Capricorn—
tradition, duty, self-
control, endurance

Jupiter in Aquarius—
humanitarian, egalitarian,
progressive, truth-seeking

Moon in Aquarius—
unconventional, sociable,
independent, altruistic

Chiron in Pisces—
the need to sacrifice, to give compassion,
ability to heal

Figure 8.1. Brief descriptions of the astrological sub-personalities in Princess Diana's chart.

Cancerian nature exhibited a great proneness to moodiness, touchiness and being easily hurt, especially when she did not find the sense of security and belonging she so craved. An astrologer would emphasize the importance of family life, of finding emotional security, and a special creative or artistic 'niche' for herself – a spiritual place – within her home and herself. An astrologer would elucidate the nature of her security needs and fragile possessiveness but also validate her fluctuating moods and their potential creativity, as well as explain how Cancerian fears can employ emotional manipulation to defend against disappointment.

Sun in the 7th house

Family life played a hugely important role in Diana's life, for she had a rich ancestral background and grew up to embrace a fate determined wholly by another powerful family – the Windsors. With her **Sun in the seventh house**, the domain of the 'other' and that which complements or completes us, we know that her own power, purpose and individuality (the Sun)

Sun, Mercury, Mars, Uranus, Pluto, N. Node 3rd quadrant

would manifest through relationships. And, of course, what proved to be the most powerful relationship was that between Diana and the British people. We look to the 1801 chart for the UK, the year of the Union or the formation of the United Kingdom, and find that its Midheaven is 9 Cancer, the exact degree of Diana's Sun. This connection between the two charts is symbolic of the important role Diana would play in influencing the future values of the country.

Diana's chart reveals six factors in the third quadrant of the chart, indicating that the impact of marriage and intimate involvement with others would be crucial for her personal development. She was painfully sensitive to the support and/or criticism of loved ones, and through her marriage to Prince Charles, her Cancerian vulnerability

Strong 7th was exposed to the world. An astrologer might
and 8th have cautioned the Princess about the pitfalls of
house this seventh-house Sun placement: becoming overly identified with and dependent on others so that she would feel incomplete without them. But at the same time, she was to find her real source of self-esteem through the healing impact she had on others in her philanthropic work.

Sun conjunct Mercury, the god of communication and language, further enhanced
Sun her capacity to speak the 'people's language', to
conjunct get her feeling message across. It was through
Mercury connection with others that she became stimulated to use her curiosity and intelligence, and eventually developed her abilities as a public speaker. But she made sure that her communications were emotionally received; she always preferred informal meetings, and liked to touch and hug those with whom she was conversing – a typical Cancerian trait. In her chart Mercury rules the sixth and seventh houses (work/health and relationships), indicating her important role as spokesperson for others. An astrologer would explore her experience of communication, and would validate her very

intuitive approach, which is also indicated by Mercury's aspects to Neptune and Pluto.

Tenderness, timidity and emotional vulnerability are only part of the Cancerian theme. Cancer also bestows tenacity, imagination and the psychic knack of understanding and influencing public sentiment. Princess Diana was intensely personal and she soon discovered her instinct for piercing through protocol to appeal to the hearts of people. Cancer is ruled by the Moon, the cosmic body that reflects solar light and which symbolizes the 'people', so we look to its position to understand further Diana's inner nature and her popular appeal.

Moon in **Humanitarian, outgoing, progressive,**
Aquarius **unconventional, independent, quietly**
(Fixed Air) **rebellious, detached, need for friendship and**
communication, group work, collective causes.

Moon in Aquarius added an independent, extrovert quality to Diana's personality, and helped to translate her sensitive, protective feelings out into the world at large. This position made her instinctively a friend of the world, and gave her a need for social freedom and experimentation, something the monarchy could not supply or allow. Though very different from each other, Cancer and Aquarius both care deeply about others but in different ways. Aquarius is airy: it needs to share ideas and ideals, it needs to feel part of an egalitarian group. Its nature is impersonal, gregarious, offbeat and zany, and strongly individualistic. It is a very principled sign, is sensitive to injustice, and believes in supporting the rights of marginalized groups.

Moon in
2nd house

Her role as friend of the needy and abused, which her trapped condition as the mythical 'princess in the tower' engendered for her, felt deeply, instinctively 'right'. Her Moon in the second house meant that her sense of self-worth was directly linked with her capacity to respond emotionally to people's needs. This lunar position also indicates that her personal resources for work and survival involved her feminine, maternal powers. Diana's work was entirely to do with the domain of feeling; she felt grounded and real when she experienced others receiving her compassionate attention and her identification with their pain. She also valued (second house) what she felt was an inalienable right (Aquarius): truthful self-expression. Her actions spoke out against the prejudices about AIDS and lepers and other emotionally explosive issues. Diana's role in the supreme archetypal family was typically Aquarian in that she was the outsider; she felt this keenly and bore it courageously. Her youth, informality and rebellious spirit had a disturbing but progressive influence on the monarchy: essentially, she brought them into the modern world. An astrologer, describing her Aquarian Moon, would emphasize her need for social mobility and independence, for communication and egalitarian friendships, her humanitarian instincts, and her need to challenge family values that were swallowed whole. An astrologer might indicate career areas which involved public service, which engaged her feisty feminine spirit, and might also suggest that she possessed inner resources of adaptability and great sensitivity to others' needs.

Moon In fact, Diana's rebellious Aquarian Moon did
opposed much more than disturb the monarchy.
Uranus Ultimately, she defied an age-old patriarchal double-standard: through her protest against an ancient norm ('marry a virgin, but keep the woman you love as your mistress') by collaborating with Andrew Morton on his biography *Diana: Her True Story*, she exposed the monarchy's exploitation of her procreative role and eventually forced them to re-examine their mores. Certainly the tragedy of her final demise brought out the full impact of her dissent, but while she was alive her Aquarian Moon was made even more rebellious through its opposition to Uranus, planet of change and deviation. This very emotionally excitable and unstable configuration gave Diana a very strong-willed and tense emotional nature which sustained her decision to challenge 'the firm' when her own role as royal consort had become an empty prison.

T-square: This Moon–Uranus aspect is also involved with
Moon, Venus, thereby forming a T-square with the two
Venus, feminine astrological deities. This describes her
Uranus emotional inheritance: at a very tender age she lost the security of mother's presence due to her

parents' divorce. The family stability was disrupted due, in part, to her mother's unconventional, strong-willed and romantic spirit. Diana inherited this same spirit, but it was an emotionally wounded and unstable spirit that craved love (Moon—Venus) but unconsciously expected rejection (Uranus). The resulting emotional insecurity could manifest, at times, in

Venus in Taurus 5th sq. Moon Aquarius 2nd, Uranus square to both

hysterical and sensation-seeking behaviour, and this in turn could make excessive demands on close relationships. Venus in Taurus gave her an earthy sensuality, possessiveness, a love of beauty, colour and luxury, and a strong power of attraction. In contrast to this was her Aquarian instinct for unusual people, philanthropy and humanitarian pursuits. This paradox was an integral part of Diana's appeal. She was both a devoted lunar mother and healer, as well as a beautiful, flirtatious Aphrodite who wanted love and adoration. The square from Uranus in the eighth house 'electrified' both feminine roles and bestowed an erratic but exciting charisma. It also brought uncomfortable and sudden lightning bolts from the most intimate part of her life: marriage and sexuality. This configuration in her chart could offer her some important insights about relationship patterns, not least of which is that the original bolt of lightning was the break-up of her parent's marriage, and that emotional healing in this area was needed.

Awareness of the fact that there were three people in her marriage brought a humiliating jolt to

Diana's sense of self-worth (Moon in the second) and to her own femininity and sexual confidence (Venus in the fifth). Although she was devoted to her sons and valued security, loyalty and family solidarity (Saturn first house), she attracted intrigue and rejection (Uranus eighth house) – a repeat of her early family experience. From a psychological point of view, it can be argued that a deep but unconscious desire to heal the painful emotional wound from the loss of her mother actually compelled her to enter a relationship with an individual who would help her re-enact the same early tragedy. An astrologer seeing this *Venus trine* problematic Moon picture would engage with her *Saturn;* on the subject of her early childhood relationships *Venus* and the way she experienced her mother. This *square* might lead to a growing awareness of the way she *Uranus* subsequently learned to respond in adult relationships; it could encourage self-reflection as to how she learned to get her emotional needs met. An astrologer would also discuss the inherent freedom-loving qualities of this configu-ration with her, pointing out that with opposi-tions there is a propensity to polarize situations and to project feelings. For example, feeling hurt when a loved one does not want to be close all the time might mean that, in fact, she does not want to be so close. The need to honour the 'spaces in-*Saturn* between' in relationships would need to be *versus* addressed; it could help her manage better the *Uranus* 'freedom–closeness' dilemma that was such a constant theme in her emotional life. The purpose of such a discussion would be to help her think about both needs: pursuing her life on her own terms (Uranus) as well as sustaining a close relationship (Moon–Venus) with someone who also needed 'space'. How to combine freedom and closeness is the challenge of her Moon–Venus–Uranus configuration.

Sagittarius Ascendant	Fiery, casual, restless, spontaneous, optimistic, freedom-loving, direct and forthright approach to life, tendency to exaggerate, sentimental, sense of anticipation, seeks meaning in all events, noble, expansive, kind-hearted.

Despite her deep loyalty to traditional family values, Princess Diana's personal style was much less conventional than that of the rest of the royal family. Certainly, this was due, in part, to her Moon–Uranus opposition, but here it is reinforced by her **Sagittarian Ascendant**. This very visible personality 'style' was warm and outgoing, restless and eager for fun. Although she needed adventure (Sagittarius), she also needed acceptance and would essentially stay firmly embedded in family values (Cancer). But the qualities she sought to develop in herself in the outer world were those of her Ascendant sign: confident self-expression, communication of passionate beliefs, and relaxed and unpretentious reaching out to others. Life placed her in a situation where these qualities were needed, and she duly set about her regal duties in a manner that was truly her own.

Sagittarius can also express itself in an exaggerated, inflated manner, and perhaps equal to her spontaneity, integrity and kindness was her self-dramatization and self-interest. Larger-than-life Jupiter rules her Ascendant; certainly its placement in the second house brought her wealth and the enjoyment of luxury and prestige. Sometimes Sagittarian pride can overstep itself and dig in its heels with a dogmatic, 'holier-than-thou' attitude. But the blessings and luck of her ruling planet, the Moon, in people-loving Aquarius, along with other more seductively charismatic qualities, made it easy for her adoring public to forgive her naive conceit. Diana valued people (Jupiter in Aquarius); despite the wealth which shielded her from the normal economic concerns of ordinary people, she had a deeply egalitarian soul and could become 'one of the gang' in almost any group she found herself with. She also saw the public as a friend, as a collective mirror who would give back what she needed – adoration and approval – and this undoubtedly helped her, during times of extreme loneliness, to continue to view her life in a philosophical, Sagittarian way, as a journey, and to see herself as a resilient participant in her life drama. An astrologer would describe this part of Diana as the restless, exuberant, optimistic traveller, or the persuasive 'salesperson' who could enthuse others and who needed to ground her vision in her work with people. She was a typically undaunted Sagittarian seeker who bounced back from problems and from her social gaffes which

Jupiter, ruler of Ascendant, in Aquarius, 2nd house

actually made her more 'real', more fallible and therefore more loveable to the ordinary person.

Saturn in Capricorn; Jupiter– Saturn conjunction

Not far from Jupiter in Diana's chart we find Saturn in Capricorn, placed on the first/second house cusp. This Jupiter–Saturn conjunction repeats and emphasizes one of the main themes in her chart: the tension between tradition, duty and the past and innovation, freedom and the future. Diana's life structure was one of privileged responsibility, rooted in a strong hierarchical tradition of noblesse oblige. Capricorn is one of the strongest positions for Saturn, giving innate discipline, self-control, ambition and a conscientious approach to work. It also gives a fierce loyalty to authority figures and a need for recognition and success. This trait is further emphasized by Saturn's square to her Midheaven, that part of the chart connected with status and one's public role. Her Venus-ruled

Saturn square Libran MC, ruled by Venus

Libran Midheaven, with Venus trine Saturn, represented her flair with people and her dedicated feminine role in supporting worthy charities. In characteristic Libran style, a large part of her role in the monarchy was seen to be that of bringing warmth and beauty and a mischievous sense of fun into formal public duties. But Saturn's aspects to her Venus and Midheaven gave a solemn, grave, dedicated edge to her work. This sub-personality could be called the 'stern father' which must have exerted a powerful 'top-dog' influence within her, making her feel acutely aware of being watched and expected to achieve impeccable standards of behaviour. The inner 'top-dog' was perfectly matched by the outer 'top-dog' – the monarchy. But this pressure to conform within a family system, where the kind of emotional sustenance she needed was in short supply, confirmed an inner sense of failure but then propelled her into a steely determination to find her own authoritative voice.

Sun Cancer versus Saturn Capricorn

Diana's Sun Cancer was her vulnerable under-belly, fluid and unformed, protected and defended by the sturdy Capricorn walls of tradition and duty. What started out as agonizing stage-fright when she found herself suddenly exposed to the world, slowly transformed itself into commanding stage presence. This is the gift of Saturn in Capricorn. But as always with Saturn, there were no short cuts to internalizing this planet's considerable strengths: through the long, cold, dark tunnels of emotional disappointment, depression and bulimia, Diana transformed chronic loneliness and self-loathing into an enduring and well-chiselled identity. She found a way to weather the emotional storms, to express her own truth, and remain devoted to her royal duties. Capricorn tradition was the painful and privileged matrix through which she made her life her own. An astrologer might open a discussion around Saturn by validating the integrity, loyalty, determination and organizational abilities this position gives, and how it enabled her to embrace the daunting challenges of her role with such commitment.

Contrasting this with her rebellious Moon–Uranus side could help her to grasp the contradictions of her nature, and help her to identify the different needs and energies within her.

The Jupiter–Saturn link with the second house indicated that self-value would be an important issue for her. It also indicated material wealth.

Jupiter–
Saturn
2nd house

Certainly, her money-earning powers were considerable while she was still alive, for her patronage was sought by many – the charities she valued attracted wealth. But, ironically, her wealth-attracting powers were only fully realized after her death in the phenomenally rapid growth of the Princess Diana Memorial Fund. An astrologer discussing this position in her chart would expound upon the strengths and defences of Saturn, and emphasize the educative value of personal experience for her development and maturity. An astrologer might also bring out the ambitious side of this position, highlighting her need for self-respect, success and recognition through finding a role in which she excelled and was admired for her contribution to the greater good. Also, an astrologer would emphasize the tension between traditional (Saturn in Capricorn) and individual (Jupiter, ruler of Ascendant, in Aquarius) values, suggesting that the scales were tipped in the direction of her need to be true to her inner heroic spirit (Sagittarius Ascendant, Moon opposed Uranus, Uranus conjunct N. Node, Venus, ruler of MC, square Uranus), however fraught with difficulties that path might be.

Jupiter
versus
Saturn

The eighth house in Diana's chart tells the deeper story of her painful transformations: Mars, Uranus, Pluto and the North Node reside here. Diana grew up in the gaze of an adoring public and transformed herself into a modern woman who knew her own power. What was the nature of this power? 'Transform' and 'power' are terms connected with Pluto, the god of the underworld. Her Sun was sextile Pluto, an aspect that gave her the energy to endure and transform painful experiences and to use them positively. Pluto's influence helped her to rise from the ashes of a destroyed marriage and self-image, fully exposed to the world, to reinvent herself. It also intensified her emotions and her will, as well as giving her the courage to face excruciating pain and difficulties in others' lives. Pluto's eighth-house position did not bode well for an easy time in marriage: this is the province of intimacy and what passes between people, suggesting that close relationships could involve power struggles, intense emotional upheaval and the breaking of taboos. An astrologer would approach this with sensitivity, and might have explained this as tremendous subterranean reserves of sexual and aggressive energy which required her awareness and which, if repressed, could erupt negatively and could prevent the happy intimacy she so craved. Mars and Pluto in Virgo suggests obsessive fastidiousness and self-criticism, as Virgo is to do with purifying, refining and improving. They also suggest the theme of health and healing, and these areas could

Mars, Uranus, Pluto, N. Node in 8th house

Sun sextile Pluto–Mars

Strong Virgo

be explored to open up positive outlets for this powerful energy.

Because Pluto is with Mars, sexuality and shared resources were a real battleground. Her basic instinctual drives were very intense, and the anger she felt at being held captive in an empty marriage and a rigid monarchy she eventually directed inwardly against herself. This was not an easy energy to manage: it is the rage of the infant, and more – Mars in the eighth can mean competition in the bedroom, and alas, the triangle she lived with had a distinctly oedipal feel to it. What is so tricky about the eighth house for anyone is the sense one has of being 'coerced' into messy situations and then blaming others, when clearly one's own emotional dynamics contrive to land one exactly in that place. And because the intensity of this position can be frightening – can feel like a life-or-death struggle – the result is usually a fanatical need to control. Mars likes to be in charge, and Pluto categorically demands it. In matters of sexual intimacy, this competitive approach is not particularly conducive to romance and marital harmony. An astrologer would look at this sub-personality – which we might call 'the revolver underneath the velvet gown' syndrome – with great care, for undoubtedly it is the most difficult configuration in her chart. It suggests an aggressive and potentially violent theme; for Diana personally, it played out as trapped sexual passion and betrayal, her own anger and revenge through revealing the truth about her intimate life, and later her courageous solo crusades for the underdog, most dangerous of which was her efforts for land-mine victims. And ultimately, it was the signature for a sudden, violent death (although this must be understood in connection with the transits she was undergoing at the time, i.e. Transit Pluto square natal Mars–Pluto–Node and natal Chiron, all linked with an eclipse).

This last statement, that Mars–Pluto–Uranus in the eighth was a signature for her sudden, violent death, needs to be more thoroughly explored in the context of Diana's life.
Mars–Pluto energy is extraordinarily difficult for any woman to express, and much more so for a woman whose life was so visibly and completely structured by the patriarchal establishment. Both astrologers Paul Wright and Nicholas Campion have identified Mars–Pluto connections in the charts of many Stuart monarchs, pointing out how the history of the Stuarts evinces their involvement in violence and anarchy in one way or another. It would seem that Diana's life fits into this larger national history in some way, that her birth chart and life show that she inherited a larger fate which constellated various painful and unresolved emotional issues for the nation. At a personal level, Mars–Pluto was very difficult for her, but in terms of the wider social dimension, Mars–Pluto allowed Diana to be an *agent of change for society*, and with its close conjunction to her North Node and placement in the eighth house,

we can surmise that her consciousness-changing role in society – the way that she brought a courageous compassion and openness to layers of society we prefer to shun – was her most important contribution. We can understand this Mars–Pluto–Uranus in Diana's chart in hindsight, and hopefully learn from her struggles to live with such a demanding energy, albeit in a highly demanding sub-culture of society. Mary Queen of Scots had a Mars–Pluto conjunction; she also had a dramatic, colourful and tragic life. Paul Wright, in his fine book *Astrology in Action*, describes her impact on Britain as belonging to 'the realm of romance and legend'. This can certainly be said of Diana.

Diana's Moon is also involved in this picture (although the aspect has a wide orb), further suggesting the possibility of self-destructive tendencies to manifest at some point. This was all the more likely to occur in a monarchist society where women (the Moon), especially the wife of the future king, have strict roles and are not encouraged to be 'potent' in typically Mars–Pluto *Mars–Pluto* ways. This is further emphasized by the Mars– *opposed* Pluto opposition to Chiron, the 'wounded healer,' *Chiron–* which in the end enabled her to learn from her *Moon* painful experiences and to become something of a 'wounded healer' for others. I hasten to add that Moon opposed Mars–Pluto–Uranus need not express itself in a self-destructive way, but it is an energy pattern that requires stringent self-awareness in order for its influence to be positive.

It is the energy of the rebel and the reformer, the person whose emotional security (Moon) was perhaps ruptured at an early age, a person who seeks out unusual relationships which awaken and shock one out of old patterns, a person who breaks through decaying rigid structures, but who must take great personal risks in order to do so. Mars–Pluto–Uranus is an energy pattern which requires tremendous courage and self-honesty. An astrologer would encourage awareness of these energies within her, emphasizing the need for conscious direction through, for example, sports and physical activity and projects to which she was passionately committed. A discussion of the nature of this eighth house configuration could alert her to any compulsions she had towards recklessness and defiantly arrogant behaviour that would mitigate against her safety and best interests. Areas of interest and possible giftedness for her would be in psychology, medicine, healing, nutrition and social work, projects that involved empowering others.

Moon and Sun, co-rulers of 8th house
Also relevant to this picture is the fact that the Moon and Sun are co-rulers of her eighth house, and are linked by a sesquiquadrate, aspect of manifestation, showing that her inner masculine and feminine sides will come together in the most creative way through the powerful cathartic change which is concomitant with intimacy.

Chiron's involvement in this configuration and its placement in Pisces allowed Diana to be a healing

Chiron in Pisces catalyst for society, to bring in a new level of social compassion, and to become an ally for other sufferers of intense unhappiness and self-mutilation. And perhaps the British people were ready for the kind of openness and honesty that she had. Her self-disclosure in the famous *Panorama* interview, rather than bursting the bubble of public adoration, actually made her 'one of us': money, beauty, position and power had not protected her from the ailments of the modern age.

Diana was often described as having 'this gift' with people. Neptune's position in her chart is symbolic of this gift, the charm, the magical aura, the glamorous shield which both protected and enslaved her. Neptune forms a grand trine with her Sun and Chiron, which is symbolic of the *Neptune in* intensely magnetic personal power she exuded. *Scorpio,* Sun–Neptune generates intense romanticism, *10th house,* idealism and a longing for a 'perfect' love. It also *trine the* gives great compassion and the capacity to *Sun and* intuitively understand the feeling needs of others. *Chiron* Neptune's 10th house placement shows that this is how she wanted to be known, this is her projected image: the compassionate, caring, giving woman. Diana also carried the projections of the nation's desire for a beautiful, benevolent queen. Neptune in the 10th suggests a romantic fixation with her father and a proneness to idealize the man (Sun) in her life. Neptune brings disillusionment to the person who is wedded to a fairy-tale dream of love; and of course, a romantic courtship and fairy-tale wedding were followed by disappointment once the honeymoon period was over. This disillusionment was extremely painful for her, and it brought about another dimension of her Neptunian role – the victim. Her public image became that of the long-suffering, altruistic princess held captive by her position in a cold, unfeeling world. Her relationship with the press, despite its agonizing, relentless intrusion, became for her a kind of last-resort tool that she learned to use well. Diana's kindness, innocence and emotional neediness may have been abused, but there was undoubtedly a complex mixture of orchestration and compliance in her role as victim. Neptune always 'muddies the water' on these issues.

Diana's aspirations were very Neptunian, and her work in the world (10th house) reflected this. Neptune's influence gave Diana an ability to 'feel with' people, to really identify with their plight, and this emotional rapport was heightened and transformed into a healing ability through Chiron's involvement with the Sun–Neptune grand trine. It is easy for Neptunian individuals to identify completely with an archetypal role, but when they do, as Jung has told us, they may suffer the inexorable fate of the archetype. Diana won sympathy and adoration from the public, and it bolstered her identity as the wronged woman. And no matter how much criticism she received for her mistakes, her 'Saint Diana' image remained intact. Her role as the Queen of Hearts

was a reflection both of her true values and of her
need for compassion and love. The whole range
of Neptune's influence can be seen in Diana's life:
her innocence, romanticism and legendary
marriage to her Sun–Neptune 'king', her glamour
and beauty, her compassion and psychic sensitivity, and her role as the sacrificial lamb. Diana
herself had said that the night before her
wedding, she felt like a 'lamb to the slaughter.
I knew it and I couldn't do anything about it'
(*Diana: Her True Story* by Andrew Morton,
Michael O'Mara Books, 1993). These are the
words of an enchanted person, someone who
walks with the conviction of a sleepwalker
entering a dream that she believes can be a
reality. This highlights the complexity of Diana's
strongly Neptunian nature, and one reason why
her public influence was so strong, for we are all
subject to intense Neptunian longings and
disappointments. She enacted some of our
deepest desires and fears. Diana gained immense
popularity and power through her Neptunian
charm, but it also exerted a power over her. An
astrologer engaging with her about this dimension
of her chart could describe the attributes of
Neptune and perhaps open up a discussion of her
feelings about her father and men in general. Her
vivid imagination would readily take to thinking
about this side of herself, but it might require
some stringent self-confrontations which could
help her pierce the bubble of a Neptunian
enchantment. This would ultimately help her to
experience less romantic disappointment as she

learned to see herself, her needs and others more realistically. And this is the challenge of a strong Neptune: allowing room for one's compassion and yearnings as well as accepting the necessary boundaries and limits of being human. Far from being a disappointing experience, accepting limits can make one feel very contained. And it is an essential step towards developing one's own creative imagination and the talents that are waiting to blossom from within.

As Shakespeare has told us, all the world is a stage and we are each 'merely players' who have a variety of roles to play in our own life drama. Over time, the plot of that drama shows itself to be repetitive in a subtle but fascinating way. Prince Diana's life was lived out on a grand stage, and so the gods come alive in a particularly colourful and mythological way. What we can gain from studying her life and chart is the realization that there were many sides, many needs, many sub-personalities within her, all vying for attention. Some of these sub-personalities were exciting and delightful, and some were very difficult and painful. We know that during Diana's life she did consult astrologers in an attempt to understand her nature better, and also, we think, to gain some hope that she could more actively participate in the transformation she desired. Throughout much of her life she may have felt like a passive victim of a predetermined destiny, but astrology shows us that this is not the case. We cannot trade charts

and lives with someone else, but we can seek to transform the difficulties in our charts into strengths, if we so choose. On the road to transformation, Diana met all the different parts of her nature. The same is true for everyone – on the road to becoming 'someone', we must encounter the 'several' and make room for them in an authentic way.

FORECASTING FUTURE TRENDS

> Those who know Astrology can only indicate in a way what will take place in the future. Who else, except the Creator Brahma, can say with certainty what will definitely happen?
>
> HINDU DICTUM

A s we have seen, astrology allows us to come to a systematic understanding of the formative qualities of time. As such it can be readily employed to analyse the potential of future times in general, and more specifically for individuals, countries and companies. It is understandable that many people feel a sense of awe and terror about the predictive aspect of astrology, for it speaks to that deep, inner knowledge within us that our control over our lives is limited. Astrologers themselves must grapple with these normal human anxieties, for being forewarned of impending 'interesting times', as the Chinese say, offers no magic wand to make Pluto go away. Some phases of our lives demand more courage and strength than others; astrology helps us to identify the timing of these phases and the meaning they may have for us.

We need to remember that 'character is destiny' and that the promise of our futures is within both the natal pattern and the mental attitude that has been nurtured since birth. It is interesting to note that some 13th-century and later Indian schools of astrology set their students the task of writing up reports on interesting times in the future. These *Nadis*, as they are called, are stored in the hereditary libraries of astrologers in different parts of India. If you visit such an astrologer he will hunt through to see if he can find a text for your date and time of birth and then read out what was written about the potential of that time many hundreds of years ago! In this sense all readings of an astrological chart are acts of forecasting the kinds of ideas that are likely to come to the fore at a particular time.

In this chapter we will be looking at what an astrologer is doing when a forecast is made, and at the various techniques that the astrologer uses to do this. These techniques can be applied to any area of life. Here we mainly limit ourselves to work with the birth charts of people, but the same principles can be applied equally to interpreting general trends, or to looking at how future patterns in the sky will impact upon countries and companies, or any other entity for which a birth chart is available.

TIME AND TIME AGAIN

In Chapter 2 we saw how the qualities of time as the 'flowing image of the Eternal' are unfolded by the planetary cycles. These cycles of the individual planets through the circle of the signs, and of each pair of planets from conjunction to conjunction, unfold the eternal round. It is therefore a relatively straightforward exercise, though one requiring a great deal of experience, background knowledge and symbolic imagination, to piece together the ways in which the ideas within a chart are likely to unfold at any particular time.

There are seven main methods used for forecasting:

- **Transits**, which relate the present positions in the sky to the birth positions.

- **Return charts**, for the moment of the return of the Sun, Moon and other planets to their position at the moment of birth.

- **Progressions**, which look at how the natal chart gradually develops or 'progresses' in the days preceding and following birth.

- **Solar Arc directions**, which look at how everything in the natal chart moves with the progressed Sun.

- **Harmonic charts** for the year, which look at how the chart 'vibrates' to the current age of the person.

- **Horary Astrology**, which sets up charts for the moment of important questions such as 'What will be the outcome of these negotiations?'

- **Dasas**, a Hindu method of looking at the life in terms of major planetary periods.

We will consider briefly each of these methods below, but first we need to look at the background assumptions of astrological forecasting.

THE FLOWER IS IN THE SEED

No matter what method of forecasting is used, it is a basic axiom of astrology that the life events in which an individual is likely to be involved are indicated in the birth chart quite as much as his or her likely personality. What 'happens' to us and how we happen to the world are two sides of the same coin. Not only 'as above, so below' but also 'as within, so without'.

The seed moment of the birth chart shows both the flower it will become and its path to flowering.

By studying what has happened to someone in the past when particular areas of the birth chart were activated by transits, the astrologer can make reasonable inferences about the kind of issues that are likely to come up at particular times in the future.

For example, an astrologer might be asked to forecast the future trends for someone who was born with a strongly placed but poorly aspected Jupiter which is being powerfully activated. The astrologer will first explain that, in general, this pattern will not only make the individual extremely optimistic, opportunistic and prone to over-extension, but also that at different points in their life they will have to face the problems which arise from uncontrolled extravagance, wastefulness and going to extremes. If the natal chart Jupiter is square Mercury and Mars in the ninth house, it is quite likely that the individual will have an incisive mind which is drawn to philosophical debate, controversy and passionate argument but also that they may be prone to get into legal disputes, and waste a great deal of energy and resources on litigation. This same pattern might equally express itself in a propensity to run into problems and accidents when travelling (ninth house matters) through carelessness and impatience. By flagging possible problems, and seeing when they may be activated, the astrologer can encourage self-reflection on this life theme which then allows the individual to take appropriate precautions.

All the world's a stage
And all the men and women merely players;
They have their exits and their entrances;
And one man (Sun) in his time plays many parts,
His acts being seven ages. At first the Infant (Moon)
Mewling and puking in the nurse's arms;
Then the whining school-boy (Mercury), with his satchel
And shining morning face, creeping like snail
Unwilling to school. And then the lover,
Sighing like furnace, with a woeful ballad
Made to his mistress's eyebrow (Venus). Then a soldier (Mars),
Full of strange oaths, and bearded like the bard
Jealous in honour, sudden and quick in quarrel,
Seeking the bubble reputation
Even in the cannon's mouth. And then the justice (Jupiter),
In fair round belly with good capon lin'd,
With eyes severe and beard of formal cut,
Full of wise saws and modern instances;
And so he plays his part. The sixth age shifts
Into the lean and slipper'd pantaloon (Saturn),
With spectacles on nose and pounch on side,
His youthful hose, well sav'd, a world too wide
For his shrunk shank; and his big manly voice,
Turning again toward childish treble, pipes
And whistles in his sound. Last scene of all,
That ends this strange eventful history,
Is second childishness and mere oblivion;
Sans teeth, sans eyes, sans taste, sans everything (Saturn).

This passage from Shakespeare's *As You Like It* (Act II, Scene 2) reminds us that there is a natural human life-cycle that runs from baby to child to adolescent to young adult, middle age, retirement and old age. Each phase of life has its purpose and dominant characteristics, which has affinities with a different planet as we have annotated above. Interestingly, Jacques' lament ends with two Saturn phases (an indication of Saturn's crucial role in incarnation?) whilst the Sun is not allocated an age as such but is the 'one man' who experiences all.

Despite the cultural changes of modern times, these ages are still relevant to us all and have been studied and plotted most recently by Gail Sheehey (a non-astrologer) in her book *New Passages* (HarperCollins, 1996). Whilst each of these progressive phases of life do not have precise ages attached, we can all recognize the loud, noisy, rebellious Mars period of adolescence and early adulthood when surly teenagers connect with their wild side, take risks, rebel against authority and experiment sexually. Major transits and progressions involving Mars during this period of life are likely to express themselves much more forcefully than, say, during old age. Likewise, major developments involving Saturn during the vulnerable years of childhood will be much more difficult to handle than in the last phase of life when Saturn comes into his own, often bringing patience, inner strength and a more contemplative attitude.

By the same token the astrologer recognizes that, for example, lunar aspects will relate to matters to do with the mother and the mothering processes of early childhood, and how the mother was experienced. And, because mother is always a primary figure in our development, it will be possible to make important deductions about significant childhood developments from the Moon's position, aspects and mid-points. So likewise a strongly saturnine chart may struggle early in life but gradually blossom with retirement, and so on.

Transits are simply the positions of the planets in the sky on a particular day. By studying how the current positions of planets relate to the birth chart it is possible to make a fairly accurate assessment, not unlike a weather report, of the current situation in a person's life. Transits are normally important in direct proportion to their speed. When a slow-moving planet, such as Pluto, Neptune or Uranus, aspects a planetary position in the natal chart, and especially by conjunction or opposition, then that planet's activities are likely to be experienced very profoundly. However, it is not the case that Pluto, for example, will be making someone 'do something', but rather the Pluto part of the outer cosmic clock will be especially tuned in to the Pluto part (and possibly other parts) of the individual's inner cosmic clock – the birth chart. Transits of these outer planets, which will often be in effect for one or two years, present opportunities for making major life changes.

The scope of this book does not allow for a detailed elaboration of all possible transits. These can be explored in the books listed in the Bibliography. However, the following brief descriptions offer a guideline for thinking about the influence of transits of Mars, Jupiter, Saturn, Uranus, Neptune and Pluto.

MARS

When Mars transits a natal planet or house, the associated areas of life will be energized, and the need to be competitive and to assert one's individuality will be activated. Mars transits help one to learn about one's personal energy and anger and how one deals with competition and conflict.

JUPITER

When Jupiter transits a natal planet or house, the associated areas of life will be given opportunities, expansion, upliftment, but there is also a proneness to take too many risks, to exaggerate expectations, and to overdo. Jupiter transits stimulate us to seek more out of life and to help our consciousness to grow, but at this time our waistline and self-importance can grow, too.

SATURN

When Saturn transits a natal planet or house, the associated areas of life will be constrained and challenged, bringing a need for us to focus careful attention on a particular part of our world. Saturn transits demand self-examination, responsibility, hard work, patience and honesty; and although often difficult and painful, Saturn's influence usually leaves us feeling stronger and wiser, with our world in a more manageable structure.

URANUS

When Uranus transits a natal planet or house, the associated areas of life will be suddenly upset and the status quo changed. The purpose of Uranus transits is to challenge rigidity, to confront complacency, to stimulate the mind, to remind us that there is no absolute stability in life, and to bring us a fresh and larger view of the world and the role we may play in it.

NEPTUNE

When Neptune transits a natal planet or house, the associated areas of life may become uncertain, confused, and prone to projections of our wildest fantasies. Neptune transits dissolve boundaries and make one extremely sensitive at many levels. It is best to 'go with the flow' and realize that we cannot come up with precise answers until this transit is over.

When Pluto transits a natal planet or house, the associated areas of life will undergo upheaval and transformation. Pluto transits bring powerful experiences which can shake us to the very core. We may try to resist the changes that Pluto brings, but we eventually learn much about ourselves through this god's cathartic and renewing effects.

SATURN'S TRANSITS

The cycle of Saturn around the chart is always an important indicator of 'where things are at'. Therefore, we will take a closer look at this planet's sojourn through its cycle. As we have seen, Saturn is the reality principle of space–time incarnation. It is the 'tester' and 'quality controller' who demands that we confront issues squarely and take stock of our performance. Saturn does two things: it slows things down so we have to concentrate all our skills on the task in hand, and it gives us an 'end of term report' when we have finished. This is especially true at the conjunctions, squares and oppositions to its natal placement in the chart. When Saturn transits our natal planets, there is always a demand that issues around that god be focused upon and given serious attention. At the time, we may kick and scream about this, but after a Saturn 'work-out' we generally feel much healthier and sometimes a little bit wiser.

So, for example, Saturn transits to the Sun challenge us to deepen our sense of focus and purpose in life and to take ourselves seriously. If we have been failing to live up to our full potential, this may be a time when we go into over-drive in order to bring some of our potential into manifestation. On the other hand, if we have been well focused, this can be a time of recognition and of reaping the rewards of our previous efforts. Saturn transits to the Moon are usually sobering; they bring

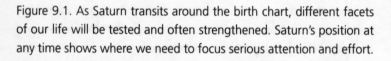

achievement in
the world

sustained work
in Society

actively seeking
outer goals

MC

10

engaging with
others

ASC

7 DESC debut into
the world

personal
tests,
withdrawal
from the
world

focus on
creativity

4

IC

rebuilding the
inner world,
domestic life

Figure 9.1. As Saturn transits around the birth chart, different facets of our life will be tested and often strengthened. Saturn's position at any time shows where we need to focus serious attention and effort.

situations that test our emotional maturity and the way we get intimacy needs met. When Venus is transited by Saturn, our social life, partnerships and aesthetic values are tested. Sometimes Saturn to Venus brings a crystallizing of the affections, so that someone who has been playing the field may establish a stable and long-term relationship under this aspect. Saturn to Mercury helps to deepen and clarify one's thinking and ability to concentrate mentally. A Saturn transit to Mars tends to focus the will and curb impetuosity, but in the process this transit can generate a great deal of friction between the individual and authority figures. Saturn to Jupiter, like Saturn to Mars, can be experienced as frustrating, but it may also help us to consolidate and develop the interests, talents and opportunities symbolized by Jupiter. With Saturn transits to Uranus we feel agitated and rebellious. This is a testing time when external situations and responsibilities challenge our own authority and independence, and sometimes the only way forward is to break with the past. Saturn to Neptune brings us down to earth, sometimes with a bump. This transit asks that we re-examine our ideals and expectations if we find that we are continually failing. Saturn transits to Pluto call us to purge our lives of structures and behaviour patterns that we have outgrown.

SATURN'S TRANSITS TO ITS OWN POSITION

Saturn's transits to its own natal position are always significant for the development of one's life. Saturn takes 29–30 years to complete one cycle. Around this age we experience the first Saturn return; the second occurs when we turn 58–59, and the third around the age 87–88. In astrological terms, 29–30 is the age at which we grow up and reach our first maturity. This period is often a watershed when we confront what is and what isn't working in our lives. We have to face the real challenges of adulthood with a more realistic attitude. This may involve the ending and/or beginning of important relationships and jobs. At the first Saturn return we have a sense of knowing ourselves well for the first time, and we feel ready to get on with our lives with renewed commitment. The second Saturn return is a period of completion when we take stock of our accomplishments and failures, and we begin to prepare for a gradual relinquishing of worldly power and concerns. The third Saturn return marks the end of life when we inwardly prepare for the final journey.

The different phases of the Saturn cycle mark important developmental stages. At about the age of 7–8, Saturn squares its natal position; it is said that at this time the child is fully

incarnated and ready for intellectual development. At the age of 14–15, Saturn opposes its natal position; at this time puberty begins. At around the age of 21–22, Saturn squares its natal position again as it begins its final seven-year sojourn to its return; at this time young people begin their first experiences of working in the adult world. As you can see, every seven years or so Saturn is aspecting its own position by a hard aspect (square, opposition, conjunction), bringing us further along our path to responsible adulthood. Along with the 28-year cycle of the progressed Moon, this movement correlates with the famous 'seven-year itch' and the tendency of many people's lives to go through significant points of crisis and change about every seven years.

SATURN THROUGH THE HOUSES

Saturn's journey around the houses of the chart shows where the 'centre of gravity' of our life is likely to be at any time. When Saturn reaches the bottom of the chart, the lower meridian or IC (fourth house), symbolically it can be a time of 'hitting rock bottom'. At this time we are ending a period of withdrawal from the world, when we have needed to focus on ourselves. This is often a very introverted phase, good for inner work, and also a time of personal consolidation when we establish the foundations for the next 29–30-year cycle. As Saturn gradually moves from the IC up the chart through the fourth, fifth and sixth houses, we focus on our creativity and work, harnessing our unique talents and committing ourselves to their development through training and practice. As Saturn crosses the Descendant and then moves through the seventh, eighth and ninth houses, our efforts to attain outer goals intensify as we engage with others in the world. The period of Saturn crossing the Midheaven often marks a time of recognition and achievement, albeit combined with fresh responsibilities. As Saturn descends through the eleventh, twelfth and then first houses, we go through a time of sustained work and achievement in society. As Saturn leaves the first house we will tend to be increasingly concerned with our personal life; this phase could even see a voluntary or forced withdrawal from previously successful work.

Thus, for example, Margaret Thatcher ascended to power as transiting Saturn climbed upward towards the Midheaven of her chart. She was elected in 1979 as Saturn reached the top of her chart, and she held the reins of power over the next 12 years. As Saturn crossed her natal Saturn and Ascendant and passed through her first house, she carried all before her, winning her third term of office in June 1987 as Saturn was leaving her first house. From this point onward she gradually met more and more opposition from colleagues, lost her grip on worldly power and was forced to establish a more private role.

A similar pattern can be seen in the case of Princess Diana. Her marriage to Prince Charles occurred on 29 July 1981 as Saturn was moving to the top of her chart. At this point she took on both responsibility and power. As Saturn moved over her Midheaven and through the fourth quadrant and then across her Ascendant in 1987, Diana became one of the most photographed and influential women in the world. Saturn arrived at the end of her first house and simultaneously returned to its natal position (her Saturn return) early in 1991. This was the point at which her isolation and separation from Charles became established and she began to withdraw from public life into her own private world. Saturn was almost exactly at the IC of her chart when her life ended so suddenly and tragically in Paris.

It should be emphasized that Saturn's descent to the IC does not suggest a violent ending of life. What it does symbolize is the end of a cycle of maturation and work in the world. Several

other difficult transits to Princess Diana's chart coincided with Saturn's movement towards her IC. At the time of her death, Pluto was transiting square her eighth house Mars–Pluto conjunction and her second house Chiron, a potentially dangerous natal configuration. The solar eclipse (a traditional forecasting marker of an important event) of 1 September 1997 was exactly on the IC through London and Paris (that is, the chart set for the moment of the solar eclipse). The degree of this eclipse fell very close to Diana's eighth house Mars–Pluto, and the MC of the eclipse fell on her Chiron. The violent energy of this combination expressed itself in a literal way as a violent accident.

PROGRESSIONS

Every day the Earth rotates on its axis. As it turns, the Ascendant and MC will pass over and, as it were, contact and catalyse every part of our chart. Progressions are based on the idea that each such cyclical unfoldment of the chart gives a preview of later cycles. As the Bible puts it, 'a year is but a day in the sight of the Lord'. In this sense the cycle of astrological experiences of the first day of life will be reflected again in the first year of life (secondary progressions) and also in the first lunar month of life (tertiary progressions). Thus if you are 30 years old, what was happening in the sky on the 30th day after your birth has a direct relationship to what will be happening in the 30th year of your life. This again suggests that life, the great time–space continuum, is in some sense a great hologram in which each part contains the whole, in which each cycle plays out the same basic story at its own speed.

In the case of Princess Diana, at the time of her marriage in July 1981, her progressed Sun had just formed an opposition to her natal Saturn. This is a classic signature for a period of settling down and taking on heavy responsibilities (Saturn) and of focusing (Sun) on an older man (Saturn) and becoming part of the Establishment (Saturn). At the same time the progressed Sun was also just 30° from Diana's Node, the point in the chart associated with major relationships. The month before the wedding her progressed Moon (feelings, intimacy) had formed an exact conjunction with Neptune, planet of glamour and romance but also of illusion and sacrifice. This progressed aspect was still in effect on the day of the wedding, and was also aligned with her progressed Midheaven. The Moon–Neptune also formed an almost exact trine to Mercury, the ruler of her seventh house of marriage. This progressed pattern vividly shows that in terms of her inner development Diana was prepared to take on a huge challenge (Sun–Saturn) in order to seek emotional fulfilment (Moon–Neptune). At the time, no astrologer could know how well she would weather the struggles and disappointments that this pattern promised. Nevertheless, Diana's progressed chart for this time aptly conveys an image of a yearning for love within a marriage of duty.

SOLAR ARC DIRECTIONS

The progressed Sun (*see above*) can be seen to mark the unfolding focus of the growing individual. The progressed Sun always retains its birth relationships with the other planets. Solar Arc directions recognize this fact and move the whole chart along by the same distance as the progressed Sun. So, if the Sun has moved through 20°, which would occur at about age 20, then all the other planets in the chart are moved by the same amount.

When a directed planet comes within about 1° orb (= about one year) of aspect to a planet or angle in the natal chart, this will begin to bring out that idea in the individual. As the aspect becomes closer so the effect will intensify.

For example, Princess Diana had just had her 20th birthday when she married Prince Charles. The progressed Sun had moved through 19° 07'. If this Solar Arc is added to Diana's Jupiter at 5° 06' Aquarius it brings it to 24°13' of Aquarius right with her Moon–Uranus–Venus T-square, the heart of her emotional life. It is applying to the conjunction of her Moon at 25°02' of Aquarius, orb 48' = about nine and a half months, the square of her Venus at 24° 24' of Taurus, orb 10' = 2 months, and separating from the opposition of Uranus at 23° 20', orb 53' = about ten and a half months.

Translated we see that over the period of her courtship and marriage, Jupiter, the ruler of her Ascendant and the traditional significator of joy, happiness and prestige, was triggering off all of her Moon-like feminine qualities, her sensual Venus in Taurus and her capacity for sudden joy. Ebertin's *The Combination of Stellar Influences*, a standard dictionary for chart interpretation, describes Moon–Jupiter as 'the girl engaged to be married, the bride'. Of Jupiter–Venus it says 'the joy of love', 'becoming engaged or marrying' and of Jupiter–Uranus 'blissful realization' and 'fortunate turns in life, a sudden change of destiny'.

At the time of Diana's death when she had found a new love her Solar Arc Jupiter was at 9° 38' of Pisces, exactly trine her seventh house Sun, orb 1' = 6 days, signature of 'joy', 'success' and wellbeing. Alas, at the same time Solar Arc Mars was at 6° 11' Libra just 8' from the exact 30° her natal eighth house Pluto with which it was in conjunction at birth. The birth conjunction indicated an attraction to violent Hades-like energy, which expressed itself in her landmines campaign.

Ebertin associates Mars–Pluto with 'violent assaults and injuries'. This pattern was further reinforced by Solar Arc Pluto at 10° 35' Libra, 54' from the square of the Sun and 32' from the 135° aspect to the Moon. Ebertin gives as a possible expression of Sun–Pluto 'martyrdom, danger to life, separation by

Providence, force majeure', and of Moon–Pluto 'inner shocks
and emotional upheavals'. This Pluto emphasis was tragically
depicted as Diana and her lover sped into the Underworld of
the Paris underpass pursued by the Furies.

HARMONIC CHARTS FOR THE
CURRENT AGE

As we saw in Chapter 5, a harmonic chart is calculated by mul-
tiplying the natal chart by the number that is wished to study.
The resultant chart shows how we 'vibrate' to that number.
Harmonic charts for one's age are based on the idea that at, say,
20 years old we will have completed 20 orbits of the Sun and
that this will 'tune' us to the idea of 20 and to our own particular expression of 20-ness in our chart. At the same time once
one is a particular age, one enters the next year. So someone
who is 20 has entered their 21st year. Hence at any one time we
are in tune with a particular number and moving towards an
understanding of the next number. So a study of both charts is
appropriate.

When using these harmonic charts to assess an individual's
present and future 'tuning' it is important to look at the dominant patterns and major aspects in the chart for the current age
and especially those involving the Sun and Moon. This should
give a broad brushstroke picture of the main tone of the year.
The major patterns and aspects in the chart for the coming year
will give some indication of the ideas and issues that will be
increasingly making themselves felt as the year unfolds.

In Princess Diana's 20th harmonic chart, three of the main
features are:

1) Sun is conjunct Saturn and in a Full Moon opposition
   Moon.

2)   The MC is on Diana's seventh house Sun and trine harmonic Jupiter and Uranus.

3)   The Ascendant is in a Grand Trine with Venus, Pluto and Chiron.

This suggests that this is a period when: 1) her life will 'come to the full' and when in some way she will need to 'get serious' about the focus of her life and probably take on heavy responsibilities, and may feel somewhat isolated; 2) her life will be focused upon (MC on Sun) happy and expansive (MC on Sun trine Jupiter) and successful relationships (Sun in seventh); 3) her approach to the world will be motivated by a sense of love and delight (Venus trine Ascendant) and passionate engagement (Venus trine Pluto) and when wounding and healing issues about relationships (Venus–Chiron) are likely to be to the fore.

In Diana's 21st harmonic chart there are three main features:

1)   Sun is conjunct Jupiter sextile the Node.

2)   Mars is conjunct the MC on her natal Jupiter and trine Venus.

3)   Mercury is closely trine Pluto with Mercury on her natal Pluto.

This suggests a year when 1) Diana would be increasingly aware of herself as a person of importance and status (Jupiter) and developing working relationships with a large number of people; 2) Diana would be very purposefully and positively focused on developing her own sense of self (Jupiter ruler of her Ascendant); and 3) Diana would be developing her powers of persuasion and focusing on her survival skills.

These taken together give a vivid picture of this remarkable time in her life when she was catapulted into the public eye and became a star overnight whilst at the same time having to take on enormous responsibilities and disciplines, and learning the skills of surviving in another world and culture.

PLANETARY PERIODS – HINDU DASA SYSTEM

It is not possible to cover the rich and separately developed Hindu, also known as Vedic, tradition of astrology in detail in this book. However, the Hindu use of planetary periods, known as *dasas*, and their sub-divisions, or *bhuktis*, is not present in the Western tradition and deserves attention. In this system, each of the traditional planets and the North and South Nodes are said to rule for a set period of years in the following sequence:

- South Node   7 years
- Venus   20 years
- Sun   6 years
- Moon   10 years
- Mars   7 years
- North Node   18 years
- Jupiter   16 years
- Saturn   19 years
- Mercury   17 years

Where in this sequence one's life starts is determined by the precise position of the Moon at birth. The power of this system is that it can identify major life shifts.

ASKING QUESTIONS –
HORARY ASTROLOGY

As outlined in Chapter 3, this is a specialist area of astrology which sets up a chart for the moment that someone asks a question, such as 'Should I sell my house?'. Using a set of well-established rules, the chart is first assessed to see if it can be judged at all. The chart is then read according to further precise rules. Such readings can throw enormous light on the back-ground to the question, the issues that are involved, and the likely outcome and possible courses to take. In the hands of a knowledgeable and sensitive astrologer, this can be a remark-able tool for unravelling knotty problems and understanding the deeper issues that lie behind them.

SOLAR, LUNAR AND OTHER RETURNS

'Many happy returns of the day', is what we say to someone on their birthday. The moment that the Sun returns to the exact degree, minute and second that it occupied at the moment of birth is, as it were, the birth of a new cycle. This is known as the Solar Return. A chart set for this moment can tell a great deal about the main issues that will come up in the year ahead. The chart is interpreted as a chart in its own right but also in rela-tionship to the natal chart. The house that the Sun is in at the Return is almost always of importance, as are any planets close-ly aspecting the Sun and any planets that are angular. A Solar Return showing Saturn setting in the seventh house of partner-ships and marriage would suggest a year in which it will be necessary to seriously work on relationships. It may also sug-gest that older and wiser people will feature in a prominent way. What this means more specifically will depend on how Saturn is aspected and its relationship to the natal chart. Of course, an understanding of the individual's present circumstances are also vital to interpretation. If the individual is single, it may suggest a year when someone will come along who makes them feel they want to settle down. On the other hand, if the individual is in a strained partnership it may indicate a 'crunch' time when it is necessary to separate or at least to acknowledge the burdens one is carrying.

The return of the Moon to its natal position each month can be looked at in a similar way. This monthly chart gives a picture of the emotional climate for the month ahead.

FORECASTING V. PREDICTING

The different methods described above will each give a different perspective on the prevailing climate. The great majority of astrologers work regularly with the first three methods and employ additional methods as appropriate.

No matter what methods of forecasting are used, it should be kept in mind that astrologers can only identify trends and processes; they cannot see 'events' as such. Just as a wise sailor works with the wind, tides and currents so likewise astrology provides us with a map of the prevailing climate. If we are aware of 'what is in the air' we can better understand what is going on and work with it. A Uranus transit over a seventh house Sun might for one person turn into the break-up of a marriage, whilst for another it could lead to a radical reassessment of the relationship and a reawakening of the marriage rather than the destruction of it.

One way of thinking about forthcoming patterns is that these various forecasting methods are showing us the curriculum for the prevailing period and which classes, opportunities and exams lie ahead. What these upcoming planetary patterns do not, and cannot tell us, is how we will use these archetypal

patterns. Given the awareness that astrology can provide, we all have the free will to work more consciously with the energies of the time and turn them, through our own choices, towards the Good, the True and the Beautiful.

LEARNING TO LISTEN –
ASTROLOGY IN EVERYDAY LIFE

All things by immortal power,
Near or far,
Hiddenly
To each other linked are,
That thou canst not stir a flower
Without troubling of a star.

O world invisible, we view thee.
O world intangible, we touch thee,
O world unknowable, we know thee

The angels keep their ancient places
Turn but a stone, and start a wing

FRANCIS THOMPSON

O ver and beyond all its obviously practical uses, one of astrology's greatest gifts is that it serves as a constant reminder that we inhabit the sacred, interconnected universe evoked by Francis Thompson.

In this penultimate chapter we look at some simple ways of cultivating our inner ears and eyes so that we can become more aware of the archetypal ideas which shape the intricacies of our individual lives no less than the great cycles of civilization and history.

With practice, you can begin to identify the archetypal creative processes outlined in this book, as they express themselves in your own life and the environment you live in.

OMENS

Oracles and omens, as author Dianne Skafte tells us, speak 'from a mysterious source beyond the personal self' (*When Oracles Speak*, Thorsons, 1997). Listening to the world of nature and human affairs for omens was taken for granted in the ancient world. Indeed, Skafte reminds us that Socrates sought guidance in this way for daily living, and when asked where these messages came from he just called them 'divine somethings'. These 'divine somethings' – messages from a source beyond ourselves – invariably are related to the 'divine somethings' called the planets.

Nowadays in the popular imagination the word 'omen' immediately conjures up images of ignorance and superstition. How could people believe that, say, the appearance of a swooping hawk at the time of a birth could presage the arrival of a future warrior? It does not seem to make any sense. Yet one of the things that astrology shows us is that there is very good reason – sound logic – for being alert to such simultaneous occurrences and for taking them seriously. Let us look at an example.

In the early hours of 20 November 1992 a fire swept through part of Windsor Castle, devastating the Private Chapel and St George's Hall. In an earlier age everyone would have seen this destruction at the very seat and inner sanctum of monarchy as a grave omen. It would have been seen to signify that the House of Windsor was in danger of 'going up in smoke and self-destruction'. The astrologer could see the story writ large in the sky: Pluto, planet of death and regeneration, was at that time passing over the Queen's Saturn-Midheaven, signifying an intensely difficult time for her and her role as the supreme voice of tradition and authority. Also at that time, Uranus and Neptune were crossing her Ascendant, bringing a dissolving, changing influence to the very face of the monarchy.

In the modern world such signs are dismissed as 'coincidences'. Anyone seriously suggesting that the fire was an indication of potentially ruinous frictions within the royal family and, by extension, within the Family of Britain, would be labelled by our culture as guilty of 'magical thinking'. How could there possibly be any connection?

And that is the crux. As long as one thinks of the universe as being shaped entirely by 'push me-pull me' material causes, it is impossible to conceive of any way for there to be a connection. But for the astrologer, who looks at the life of the cosmos in terms of formal causes, such seeming coincidences are reasonable, to be expected and indeed anticipated.

Once we realize that life is essentially meaningful and constantly speaking to us of our relationship with those 'divine somethings', much that seems like odd or meaningless coincidence suddenly becomes intelligible. When Margaret Thatcher slipped on the steps of the Imperial Palace in Peking as she was leaving the final negotiations over Hong Kong, those with eyes and ears for such things knew all was not well. This time the Iron Lady had 'slipped up'. When we look at her astrocartography for Hong Kong (that is, her birth chart set for that place), we see that her natal Uranus is angular (near the Ascendant). Her Mars sets near Peking, revealing that this is likely to be an awkward and upsetting area for her, where her power (Mars) tends to be in the hands of others, and there is a far greater risk of sudden (Uranus) problems and defeats at the hands of opponents (Mars in seventh).

One more example. During 1997 the UK (yes, remember countries have charts, too) was to experience Pluto moving square its own Pluto position. This indicates a time of major transformation and transfer of power. So when red roses were reported freakishly bursting into bloom in Scotland on 1 January 1997, those who were listening with inner oracular hearing heard the impending defeat of the true blue Conservative Party, expressed eloquently with flowers. In fact, they lost every single seat in Scotland. And when, shortly after that, John Major was obliged by circumstance to call a general election on 1 May, 'Labour Day', the symbolism of impending Labour landslide victory could hardly have been more self-evidently written on the calendar. Pluto's coming changes were well confirmed before the event.

The formative principles of the cosmos are constantly expressing themselves at every level. When you have learned and truly internalized the astrological symbol system, you can use these 'divine somethings' as guides or springboards to more fully understand what is happening in your own inner–outer life. Outer events are constantly mirroring inner processes. Indeed, 'inner' and 'outer' are essentially parts of one another. For in reality, in the unity of things, it is impossible to draw an absolute line between our inner consciousness and our outer relationship with the world.

LISTENING TO THE ELEMENTS

The four elements – Fire, Earth, Air and Water – are seen and experienced in the world around us all the time. The seasons contain our spiralling journey through life. Sometimes we bask in the glory of spring sunshine; other times we have to 'battle the elements'. Ancient peoples lived in an 'ensouled' world where the elements of nature were alive and communicating all the time. In fact, the more we deliberately explore and engage with the elements, the more we can appreciate their deeper unique significance for us.

In the case of Windsor Castle, we saw Fire in its most terrifying and destructive form. There was something of the 'fires of Purgatory burning out corruption' about this event. Fire can certainly be devastating. It can also be the most powerful and creative of all the elements. After all, the Sun is the source of 99.9 per cent of all energy. From energetic muscles burning calories to car engines and jet planes burning fuel, we witness the force of Mars propelling things forward. In the blacksmith's forge it is the heat which allows the iron to be shaped. In the garden we observe plants begin to grow and flourish with the coming of warm spring days.

Most of us also flourish in the sunshine or in front of a roaring fire. Lighting a match and watching it consume the wood, or studying a candle's flame and the way it leaps upwards to consume anything flammable, or watching the fire on a stove slowly transform ingredients into a nourishing, delicious meal – these exercises enable us to engage with the element of Fire. A lack of fire in the birth chart can manifest as a lack of enthusiasm and little trust in life. How does Fire make you feel? Are you more aware of its threatening, transformative properties, or its warming, creative side?

Earth is where we live, where we are grounded. Earth is the raw material of our world. Walking in the mud, or digging the garden, or undertaking any kind of building work puts us in touch with the nourishing solidity and fertility of Earth. Earth is also our body and therefore the routines that keep it going. Earth is about the 'nitty gritty'; it is about being solidly practical and 'down-to-earth'. If you are someone who tends to go around with your feet 'three feet off the ground', it is an excellent exercise to walk bare foot and feel the earth under your

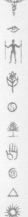

feet, and to buy plants and look after them. Equally it is good to connect with your material wellbeing by keeping accurate accounts of your daily expenditure, no matter how boring and tedious that may seem. The power of Earth can suddenly turn destructive in landslides and earthquakes. During earth catastrophes, we are terrified that the very foundations of our lives are crumbling. People who 'fly from Earth' can deny their bodies; they may eat very poorly and avoid anything 'heavy', so it may also help to eat potatoes and other root vegetables which grow in the earth. Too much Earth in your life can lead to sluggishness, to getting 'stuck in a rut' and to feeling heavy and burdened with responsibilities. In this case, a bit of unpredictable Fire can help you 'lighten up'.

Air is invisible, yet without it we would die in minutes. Air is all-pervasive, constantly moving, and connects us with everyone everywhere. Deliberately taking deep breaths of fresh air in the morning and savouring it can add an instant sparkle to the mind. Walking in the wind and feeling the breeze upon your face 'blows cares away'. All sound, be it of grunts as in primitive communication, or profound, eloquent speech, or music expressing the language of the soul, is carried through the Air. Air types 'breeze in and out' of rooms with bright salutations. Listening to yourself speak as a series of sounds and listening to languages you do not understand can connect you to the essence of communication. Freud discovered the power of the 'talking cure' – no accident there, with his Moon and Saturn in the Air sign Gemini. Likewise music of all kinds encourages a connection with Air as does smelling the scents of flowers on the breeze. 'Sound pollution' is a modern affliction which has made us all more aware of this element. We need our 'sound space'! Air is always related to intellect, but witnessing a tornado or hurricane reminds one of the sheer power of the element which can drive windmills and carry boats and balloons across vast distances. Wind storms express a kind of madness of the rational function. Too much air makes us dry and impersonal, but without those times when we 'throw open the window' to let in fresh air, we become stale and closed in on ourselves.

Water is the element of emotion and feeling. Walking in the rain, or sitting by the sea and simply listening and being with the element of Water, can be very emotionally healing. Water flows, dissolves, unifies, purifies. Becoming aware of the way water flows and eddies, filling to the level of its container, always taking the path of least resistance, helps us understand the Water type of person. They follow their feelings, they adapt to their emotional needs. And lest we think of Water as producing ineffectual 'drips', we need only remember how the power of a constant tiny flow can erode and wear down a stone; how the pounding seas can devastate and swallow, and how piped water can drive a turbine, to recognize that Water power is as formidable in its own way as Fire power. Lack of Water can produce a dryness of being, and a shrivelling up of the spirit. Simply standing in the shower or soaking in the pool or a bath both cleanses you of physical dirt and of the psychic contamination of your environment. Being in water can also allow you to 'let go'; it can connect you with your feelings about yourself and the world. Having a good cry releases a flood of feeling; it dissolves hardened attitudes and soothes broken hearts. What is your feeling about rain, the sea, swimming, bathing, being with water?

Every plant or tree we encounter is, like ourselves, a constant interplay of all the elements. It starts life as an 'air' idea: the DNA in its seed, its blueprint. The seed then works with the Sun and Water to transmute the nutrients of the Earth into its desired body. The right amount of each element is required for the seed to grow, but if you are a desert cactus you need a lot less water than if you are a grain of rice in the paddies of

Thailand. The same is true for human beings: we each have a unique blueprint, each with a unique attunement to the elements. A person with very little water may need to be by the sea more than a typical water type; a fiery individual often needs to get his feet into the soil. We can address our elemental imbalances through our enjoyment of nature – and through our relationships with others who are 'opposite' to us.

PEOPLE-WATCHING

Happily for the student of astrology, our society is fairly obsessed with the famous, not least actors and actresses and public figures. And since astrologers are equally fascinated by people and are constantly publishing the birth data of the famous, it is possible to learn an immense amount of the stellar art and science by studying the stars of stage and screen.

Sometimes the dominant planetary energy in an individual's life and personality is obvious. Take the tennis champion John McEnroe, nicknamed 'superbrat' because of his volatile temper. Here Mars is expressing itself through his choice of career – the sportsman – and also vividly through his hot-tempered character. In fact, the volume of competitive, go-getting Mars is turned up very high in his chart through its square to Pluto and conjunction with his Moon. Winning becomes a do-or-die activity for Mars–Pluto types, and whoever obstructs his goal gets to feel the full power of his infant rage!

Susan Sarandon is a lunar type: the Moon exactly rises in earthy, decisive Capricorn. Note her large, sorrowful, empathic, hypnotic eyes, the simultaneous mysteriousness and simplicity of her smile. The angularity of the Moon is a signature of powerful goddess energy, and sure enough, she is a goddess-actress who has portrayed the whole spectrum of the female experience: the nun in *Dead Man Walking*, the wild feminist in *Thelma and Louise*, the devoted mother in *Lorenzo's Oil* and even Marmie in *Little Women*. Of course, the attributes of that powerful Moon are further augmented by her Sun conjunct Neptune, allowing her to go inside a character and bring out an intimate presence that lures one into her world.

And then there is Madonna. No mistaking what goddess is running the show with this megastar. Venus in Leo square Neptune in Scorpio is the cosmic shorthand for her intensely seductive and self-dramatizing style. This is Aphrodite incarnate, enjoying her sensuality and the audience it commands to the full. Her Leo Sun's desire to capture the world's attention is supported by this position. But interestingly, it is her serious Virgo Moon and Ascendant (trine a very physical Mars in Taurus – the stuff of 'material girls') that have sought to bring to perfection her goddess aspirations. Intense physical training and stage orchestration are part of Madonna's key to success.

Another powerfully charismatic Leo is US president Bill Clinton, but in his case it is a sexually-charged Mars configured with slippery Neptune and both exactly conjunct his Libra Ascendant. Two lots of planets in Leo and Libra, both sociable and extrovert signs, account for his popular appeal and his high ideals, but his angular Mars–Neptune indicates the proneness to allow poor judgement and a love of risk to sabotage his public image. Moon in sensual Taurus, also in aspect to Mars–Neptune, further emphasizes his erotic appetite and the likelihood of his demise coming through sexual scandal if he allowed himself to get caught in the power-is-the-ultimate-aphrodisiac game. Seeing these potentials, an astrologer (if Clinton had sought one) might have strenuously advocated a boundaried, discreet approach to all relationships and a focus on his Saturn in the tenth house responsibilities. Alas, the womanizing side of Jupiter–Zeus in the first house so often makes one feel immune to the earth-bound laws of human society.

Woody Allen is even more complicated. One of the world's most famous jesters, Allen is a brilliant combination of the social satirist, the comic and the philosopher. He has that classic Sagittarian instinct of the good story-teller: he knows what part to exaggerate, what to leave out, and has a great sense of timing. Not only is he a Sun Sagittarian, but his Sun is also conjunct larger-than-life Jupiter in that planet's own sign. His films usually explore his fiery, Olympian fantasies contrasted with the disappointments and tedium of reality. Enter Saturn in Pisces, the source of his chronic angst. Saturn and Jupiter form a square in his chart, showing that each struggles for supremacy: virility and optimism versus defeat and pessimism. His love-life and claim to writing his own moral code on same is legendary; love, passion and adultery are also major themes in his films. So, not surprisingly, he also lives with a Venus–Mars–Pluto T-square, the stuff of Anthony and Cleopatra–type relationships.

No-one can watch the film actor Jack Nicholson without sensing an extremely mixed bundle of messages. He is a tense combination of solid, sensual Earth and volcanic, volatile Fire. He often plays the uptight, wounded misfit (Moon in self-critical, modest Virgo exactly opposite Saturn in Pisces), and yet is also very much at home playing a very violent, sensual and threatening character. His Venus on the Midheaven in Aries closely square Pluto, god of the Underworld, in the 12th house exactly opposite expansive Jupiter tells us he has a huge appetite for women and romance, and is happy acting in the seductive Dionysian role. These two images – Moon–Saturn and Venus–Pluto–Jupiter – suggest very ambivalent feelings about women, and they create an extremely colourful, passionate but unstable and emotionally explosive combination. At the same time he has the Ascendant in Leo, giving a certain superior arrogance, in square to an elevated Sun and Uranus, creating a tension and 'wait for the explosion' quality about his presence and

appearance. Taking an even closer look, the ambiguity of his
sexual energy is compounded by the fact that the mid-point of
his passionate Venus in Aries and his Mars in fiery Sagittarius is
configured with his Moon–Saturn, that place in himself where
he is most repressed and contained. Uncomfortable indeed!

If you decide to study astrology, do invest in some volumes
of astrological charts such as the collections of charts by Lois
Rodden or Hans-Hinrich Taeger. These are increasingly available on CD for direct use on your computer, which is of course
the ideal way to quickly get to the essential details of any chart.

APPEARANCE

Appearance literally means 'coming into view'. How people
appear, their physical make-up, walk, gestures (or lack of gestures), facial expressions and general manner can reveal a great
deal about the dominant planets and signs in their chart. And
whilst one should be cautious about drawing too many definitive conclusions from simple outward appearance, it is an
invaluable way of exercising one's understanding of astrological principles.

The American novelist Henry Miller, author of *Tropic of Cancer* and *Tropic of Capricorn*, wrote a biography of Henri Moricand, a French astrologer who had trained himself to a very
high degree to recognize the subtle differences in outer style
and self-presentation. Moricand was able to walk round a party
of people and, after a few minutes, tell each of the guests the
probable year, date and even time of their birth.

As in any other area, 'practice makes perfect'. Start with the
charts of people you know. Try to detect the ways in which the
Ascendant and other dominant features of the chart express
themselves. The key is to tune in with 'inner seeing and hearing'. You can learn a great deal by studying your friends and
family and people in the news.

The **Sun** and the sign Leo on an angle, especially the Ascendant or Midheaven, bestow a warm, noble quality. When you meet people with an angular Sun, you just know you are in the presence of a great being or a megalomaniac. Like the Sun, they must shine, they must 'follow their bliss', and that means nothing less than following their own interests and aspirations, their most creative bent, with an unwavering zeal and commitment. This is the Apollo type, radiant and benevolent in their attempt to harmonize the world. Although they can be inflexible, autocratic and bossy, something about them – their leadership qualities and their genuine desire to find their highest potential – usually lets them get away with it (unless the Sun is in hard aspect to Uranus or Pluto when their authoritative bearing becomes more tyrannical). A large, open-wide face with a wild mane of hair characterizes this type. There is often apparent a kingly presence: the way they carry themselves, the fanatic gleam in their eye, the sense of enjoyment they have in being themselves, their lack of any hint of subservience. But what they do serve is some ideal which they assume will illuminate, invigorate and improve their own little province of the world. Sometimes these types have such intense creative energy that they find it difficult to rest, to turn off. They are forever living in the future which is already planned out in their minds. Paul McCartney has Sun conjunct the Midheaven. He is a true son of Apollo who hears the music and must play it.

The **Moon** and the sign Cancer on the Ascendant give a rather shy but extremely personable style of relating. Being able to respond in a way that makes people feel both seen and soothed is what makes these people so popular, even though they would say they hate crowds and may even suffer from agoraphobia. Lunar types are very moody. Just like the tides, sometimes they have to retreat, roar with laughter or wail without explanation. Ultra-sensitive to what is going on and being said, they will go back into their crab-like shells if they feel threatened or even offended. They often have funny-shaped bodies and utterly beguiling smiles. They guard their families and privacy jealously and feel bereft without something or someone to fuss over. Susan Sarandon, already mentioned as an angular Moon type, is a devoted mother who won't let the press anywhere near her young brood.

Venus and the signs of Taurus and Libra strong, especially on the Ascendant or Midheaven, tend to make people 'attractive' in a charming and sensual way. Famous beauties like Brigit Bardot and Marilyn Monroe have a strong Venus. John F. Kennedy and Bill Clinton are classic Libra Ascendant types – witty, charming, good-looking, diplomatic. Aphrodite-ruled people are constantly seeking to engage in relationships. Aphrodite is flirtatious and seductive with a melodious voice; she always wants to look good and is rarely unaesthetic. Her vice is vanity and the desire to make another sexual conquest with little thought of the consequences. Morals are not an Aphrodite thing; love, beauty and pleasure make her tick. Bill Clinton is typical in this respect. Michael Douglas, who had to go into an addiction clinic because of his compulsive promiscuity, has Sun, Neptune, Mars and Venus all in Libra, one of the most hypnotically sexual combinations one could have. A Scorpio Ascendant adds to his emotionality and intense compulsion to become embroiled in tempestuous liaisons.

The youthful **Mercury**, or Gemini–Virgo Ascendants, gives a wiry, alert, but somewhat nervous appearance; often lean and androgynous looking, studious and interested, with agile, funny facial movements. Mercurial types are good talkers, charming and witty, move quickly in and out of situations, and when they finally settle, their brains are still ticking away – they can be in two places at once. Talking on the phone, watching television and doing homework all at the same time is no

problem for Mercurial types. It's hard for Virgo Rising to stop working, or at least feeling he should be working, so a worried, pensive brow on the face of a demure, neatly dressed person is a dead giveaway for this type. You can almost see and feel the Mercury Ascendant type's brain clicking into gear when you meet him: is there a problem he can solve for you? Something to analyse or fix? He's very busy and impatient, so speak up or he'll get bored, or feel useless, which is even worse. Tony Blair has Gemini Rising, with Mars right on the Ascendant: he is bright-eyed, powerfully alert, and a gifted talker in his famous 'sound-bite' (Mars!) sort of way.

Mars types, with a strong Mars and/or Aries or Scorpio Ascendants, are also easily recognized: intense, forceful, self-centred with a 'thrusting-ahead-so-if-you-don't-mind-get-out-of-my-way' feel, they are the pushy 'me first' people who seem oblivious of anyone else's existence. Life is a competition for these types, and if they aren't battling their way towards a desired goal, they wonder what the point of it all is. Their commitment and energy can inspire, so they make natural leaders, although it is not usually command over others that they seek, but rather a sense of their own potency and effectiveness on their environment. Still, they can be bolshy and spiky if anyone gets in their way. Scorpio Ascendant is less obvious: they survey the scene and keep their conclusions to themselves. Later on, when no one is looking, they make their move. Whilst they hold themselves back at first encounters, all the while their stance is saying 'dare me to move!'. They are enigmatic, and have a buzzy, magnetic sex appeal.

Jupiter, Almighty Jove, was the king, so not surprisingly those with a strong Jupiter, or Sagittarius Ascendant, are 'larger than life', in both body and spirit. These types have a kind nobility about them, and are prepared to give others the benefit of the doubt. They come in distinct types, though both may exude a mixture of confidence and arrogance. The 'jovial' type can be enormously good natured, 'trendy', a bit clumsy with a loud laugh and a back-slapping camaraderie. A wide, open face with ready grin invites others into their orbit: strangers are just new friends to them. The other type is more serious, philosophical and morally earnest, the judges and priests of society, but nevertheless just as benevolent. They need to know how everything fits together to create 'justice for all'. Jupiter types can exaggerate wildly and may be very concerned about wealth and status. But when it comes to the crunch, they always make choices that fit with their conscience – they simply couldn't live with themselves otherwise.

Saturn types, meaning those with Saturn angular or Capricorn Ascendant, often have a strong, fine-boned, well-chiselled face, and there is usually something quite melancholy about the eyes. They have known sadness, grown up too soon; and yet, that sadness has a beauty and strength which makes others feel at ease, completely safe and secure. If, however, Saturn receives difficult aspects from Pluto, a harsher, more defensive expression can be seen. This type often wears formal or conservative clothes, dark colours, is very controlled and dignified, but also can be very funny and insightful when in the mood. Sometimes this type is completely rational and difficult to get to know. They expect life to be hard, so in social situations it can take quite a while to warm them up, get their guard down. If you really get to know them, they may share some of their hard-earned pearls of wisdom with you. Well worth the wait.

If **Uranus** is angular, or Aquarius rises, there is a distinctly zany, cool but friendly style. This is the type that defies the very thought of classification: they are the original 'one-offs' of the zodiac. Often very cerebral with a bright-eyed-bushy-tailed look, this type can be a bit mad professor-ish, with hair standing on end as though struck by lightning or an electric shock, like Doc in *Back to the Future* who thinks up ways to drive in and out of the time tunnel. For this reason, they need to avoid electrical sockets! These types require space but are still true-blue friends. Incredibly principled, they fight the good fight on behalf of everybody, but often find it hard to know what's best for themselves – in a practical or emotional sense. They are a law unto themselves, and often discover important cosmic laws, like Albert Einstein who had Uranus as a handle to his chart.

Angular **Neptune** types, and those with Pisces Ascendant, have those dreamy, round, emotional faces which invite you into the deep blue sea of their minds. Shy, sweet, sometimes pathetic, sometimes ecstatic, these people are walking poems and are not to be 'understood' rationally. They are extremely sensitive and so need to be very careful about the people they befriend and the environment they inhabit. They may lure you into their romantic world, and why not – it's a beautiful place. But they can suddenly disappear, too, and just as with the Little Mermaid, you shouldn't ask where they've gone. Neptune bestows psychic sensitivity, imagination and a tendency to blur boundaries and give inaccurate interpretations of reality. These people can sometimes feel like their bodies aren't their own; they are mere channels for something else. They need to be gently reminded that, yes, those are their bodies, and bodies live in the real world. Neptune types have a playful sense of humour, tremendous insight, and often a heightened receptivity to spiritual experiences.

The **Pluto** type, and those with Scorpio rising, have an intense stare that says 'I see right through you; and I dare you to look at me'. Dark, brooding eyes that check out where all the exits are. This is the Godfather, controlling the whole show from behind the scenes, or the magician-alchemist who knows how to transform his world. If Pluto is rising, he knows he must transform himself, but he's afraid someone is going to do it for him. Silent, controlling, tenacious, mysterious, this type is a natural psychologist whose understanding of deeper forces can be used either positively or negatively. Intensity is the key characteristic. If Pluto walks into the room, face your fears and tell the truth; otherwise, you invite this individual's x-ray vision, and it can be uncomfortable. The actor Al Pacino has Pluto Rising; he is famous for his roles in *The Godfather* and other films, as well as his exceptionally fine performance in *The Scent of a Woman* where his coal-dark eyes appear to have x-ray vision, but in fact it is the power of his nose that picks up all the important information about a person.

CHILDREN

Astrology's insights can help parents raise children wisely. Looking at a child's birth chart introduces a healthy distance and respect for a little soul who is a separate person with distinct talents and purposes. Even though parents may insist that of course they know their children are different than them, there is nothing quite like peering into that mysterious mandala, your child's birth chart, to bring home that reality.

But particularly helpful is the way the birth chart reveals the kinds of inner conflicts and fears a child is likely to have, and the way he or she may cope with them. For example, difficult Mercury–Saturn aspects in a child's chart indicate fears about intellectual inadequacy and being 'stupid'. Saturn may slow down or delay proficiency in reading or communication, but by and large it will also deepen the mind and give an intellectual appetite for thoroughness which, in some cases, makes these children seem much older than their years. Understanding this side of their child's nature can help parents realize what is really going on when Johnny becomes unduly anxious about reading or worried about how he may perform at school. It also lets parents know what he needs – no inappropriate pressures or guilt trips about homework, and plenty of relaxed support.

Likewise, understanding the differences and connections between the charts of parent and child can help relationships improve – if the parent chooses to make the effort. For example, a parent has the Sun and Saturn in efficient, discriminating Virgo forming a square to her daughter's Sun and Uranus in warm-hearted, spontaneous Sagittarius. The daughter's innate nature is outspoken, freedom-loving, restless, clumsy, anarchic, but friendly and idealistic too. Mother's nature is much more controlled, dutiful, critical. Her daughter's personality may easily, at times, be a real challenge and make the mother respond even more like a policeman (Saturn) than she inwardly wants to be. Saturn likes structure, Virgo likes rules; Uranus likes freedom, Sagittarius does, too. A conflict between different ways of being could cause unnecessary anxiety for both, but if mother takes the time to understand her daughter's astrological make-up, she can begin to cultivate a tolerance for a different world-view, different needs, a different way of being. She can learn a lot about herself in the process, too.

ASTROLOGY AND DREAMS

Much has already been said about the birth chart as a tool for understanding our conscious, observable personality. But the birth chart is a reflection of the entire psychic life of an individual, and as such it can be very helpful when exploring the strange and beautiful symbolism in our dreams. Through the activity of dreaming we explore uncomfortable feelings and dilemmas, longings and fears, which we experience as indigestible in waking life. Messages and insights 'come' to us only if we respect the dream and enter its other-worldly truth.

During a period when the outer planets – Uranus, Neptune and Pluto – are making major transits to our chart, these gods may bless us with a gift, a powerful image in a dream, which may offer a kind of way forward, or at least a way to think about the potential meaning which that transit has for us. To explore this very rich potential of astrology, besides having a basic knowledge of your chart and current transits, you will need to make a dictionary of symbols your constant companion. An excellent book to read on the subject is Linda Reid's *Crossing the Threshold: The Astrology of Dreaming* (Penguin Arkana, 1997).

HOW AM I FEELING?

As we now know, it is not possible to separate our emotional wellbeing from the state of our physical health. Disease means a lack of equilibrium, an entity having fallen out of harmony with itself and its environment for some reason. Illness can be caused by deficiencies of various kinds, such as specific nutrients, healthy living conditions, physical affection, as well as by different kinds of stress which, over time, cause actual damage to cells and organs. The birth chart, as a picture of the whole person, will reveal likely areas where imbalance and stress may take their toll. Through an understanding of our birth chart, we become more intimately familiar with our emotional and physical weaknesses and the way our unique mind–body connection works. The birth chart particularly encourages us to take a more holistic view of our health needs, and this in turn makes us more responsible for the choices we make, such as what we eat and drink and how we approach work and play.

In medieval times all doctors were astrologers. Few allopathic doctors today use astrology to understand the suffering of their patients, and this is understandable in a world which looks at symptoms as bits to be 'fixed'. But becoming an astrologer means that you have at your disposal a tool by which to understand the correspondences between your psychological and physical state. The field of medical astrology is growing steadily as practitioners from various healing disciplines are drawn to astrology as a diagnostic guide. However, it must be emphasized that there are very few medical astrologers indeed who can, or would, predict future illness based on the birth chart. That approach causes unnecessary anxiety, and it is always very difficult to know whether an energy pattern will express itself at the somatic level or the psychological level. Where astrology is helpful is in providing an overall view of a person: their elemental bias, the energy flow through the planetary aspects, dominant energies through angularity, and then the stresses the chart may be experiencing due to transits.

For example, the Moon in the chart relates to the digestive system, to the way we nurture ourselves both emotionally and nutritionally, and to our security needs. When depressed, some people eat, and others stop eating. Both responses to depression can affect one's health adversely. If you are feeling depressed over a period of time and you know that Saturn is transiting your Moon, whatever course of action you choose – anti-depressants, psychotherapy, tearing your hair out, sleeping all day, or quitting your job and going on holiday – you are fortified with insight about what is happening. Apart from knowing that it will not last forever (Saturn will move on), this knowledge allows you to use the experience in a potentially constructive way. Saturn constricts; its transit to the Moon will pull you into yourself, perhaps making you feel cut off from people, isolated, unloved, feeling as though life is all work and no play. If you rush to the fridge you can think 'will stuffing myself with food really make me feel better, when what I really want is love?' If you lose your appetite for food and life, you can think 'here I am, all on my own; who am I? What do I really want and need?' In other words, Saturn depression can become a profound meditative experience which focuses on your lunar nature, that inner, feminine, relational self which at this time may need some therapeutic, maturational work. This approach honours the fact that underneath the seeming random trials and tribulations of living there is a pattern of self-development, there is meaning to the madness – if we but engage with ourselves, our symptoms and the symbols of the heavens. From this point of view, symptoms are only another form of omen, the mind of the body telling us what's wrong.

ASTROLOGICAL RESOURCES

Having read this far you may have decided that you want to study astrology yourself, or that you want to have your own chart done. Below are details of:

- where to find out more about the world of real astrology;

- some of the main schools offering classes and correspondence courses;

- how to find a consultant astrologer;

- some computerized astrology reports and what they offer.

A KEY RESOURCE

The annual yearbook *Astrology*, produced by The Urania Trust, an Educational Charity (Number 313780) which is dedicated to the advancement of the knowledge of real astrology throughout the world, is an invaluable resource. *Astrology* is normally published in December each year for the year ahead and is available in all the central reference libraries in the UK and in key libraries around the globe. The main contents are also available at the UT web site: http://urania.org

Astrology contains up-to-date details of all the major schools, organizations, societies and groups throughout the world. It also includes invaluable details of astrological libraries, bookshops, software and computer services, international conferences and events, journals, publications and publishers and of the major web sites and other essential information about specialist areas of astrology and astrological resources. A condensed ephemeris gives the position of the Sun, Moon and planets for the following two years and much else. *Astrology* is available directly from the address below priced £5 (including postage), or £6 including postage anywhere in the world.

The Urania Trust
396 Caledonian Road
London N1 1DN
Tel: 0171–700 0639
Fax: 0171–700 6479

The Astrological Association of Great Britain
Unit 168
Lee Valley Technopark
Tottenham Hale
London N17 9LN
Tel: 0181–880 4848
Fax: 0181–880 4849

The AA, as it is commonly known, is the other major resource for news and information about astrology in Britain and worldwide. It publishes three major journals *(see below)*.

STUDYING ASTROLOGY YOURSELF

If you want to take your studies further, contact:

The Faculty of Astrological Studies
54 High Street
Orpington
Kent BR6 0JQ
Tel: 07000 790143
Fax: 01689 603537

Founded in 1948, it is the oldest and most highly respected teaching body for astrologers in the world. It has graduates and correspondence students at both Certificate and Diploma level in almost every quarter of the globe. The FAS also runs some day and evening classes in London and a Summer School every August at Jesus College, Oxford. Its qualification, 'D.F.Astrol.S.', Diploma of the Faculty of Astrological Studies, is recognized internationally as representing a high level of overall astrological competence, whilst its two year post-Diploma Counselling in Astrology course leading to the R.C.Astrol. (Registered Counselling Astrologer) is a higher level qualification for those who wish to practise as counselling astrologers. The FAS Diploma examinations are open to all students, whether they have studied with the Faculty or not. Successful candidates are allowed to use the letters D.F.Astrol.S. after their name.

The Mayo School of Astrology
(Principal: Jackie Hudson, D.M.S. Astrol.)
Alvana Gardens
Tregavethan
Truro

Cornwall TR4 9EN
Tel: 01872 560048
email: jackie.h@virgin.net

This school grew out of the Faculty of Astrological Studies. It has its own training programme which is run on similar lines to that of the FAS. It issues Certificates and Diplomas to its own students on the basis of continuous assessment during the course together with written exams.

The English Huber School of Astrological Counselling
PO Box 118
Knutsford
Cheshire WA16 8TG
Tel/fax: 01565 651131
email: huberschool@btinternet.com

This is a UK branch of the Zurich-based Astro-Psychology Institute founded by Bruno and Louise Huber. It teaches a systematic course in astro-pyschology through correspondence courses, seminars and residential workshops which brings together astrology and the psychosynthesis approach to psychology and counselling of the late Roberto Assagioli. It awards a diploma, Dip A.P.I., which is issued in Switzerland after both written exams and a personal assessment.

The Centre for Psychological Astrology
BCM Box 1815
London WC1N 3XX
Tel/Fax: 01227 362427
email: admin@coad.org.uk
website: http://www.astrologer.com

The Centre issues a limited list of those of its graduates who also have other counselling or therapeutic qualifications.

CHOOSING AN ASTROLOGER

Astrologers undertake a wide range of work. The 'General Practitioner' astrologer of the kind produced by the Faculty of Astrological Studies will have a broad understanding of all the different branches of astrology from counselling and psychological to mundane, horary and electional.

ASTROLOGICAL QUALIFICATIONS

As in any other area, it is usually safer to seek out a practitioner who has subjected themselves to some formal training under the supervision of an organized school. Not only does this give some assurance that the practitioner has a thorough grounding in astrology, but it also means that they will have signed a code of ethics. Should anything go wrong with your consultation, you will have a professional body to which to turn for redress.

CONSULTANT LISTS

Most of the main schools issue their own list of consultants that it considers sufficiently qualified.

In addition, the Association of Professional Astrologers (APA) publishes a list of its members. Membership is limited to those astrologers who can demonstrate that they have either appropriate diplomas and/or other training and experience which issues from various sources, including the internet. Write to: The Secretary, 80 High Street, Wargrave, Berkshire RG10 8DE.

As in other areas of therapy, it is usually most satisfactory when you can find someone who knows the work of an astrologer and can recommend them. This is both to ensure that the work is of an acceptable level, and that you are likely to be on the same wavelength.

UNQUALIFIED ASTROLOGERS

Qualifications should not be your only criteria when choosing an astrologer. Astrology attracts some very independent-minded souls who shy away from organized astrology. Amongst them are many fine astrologers with years of experience.

COMPUTERIZED ASTROLOGY REPORTS

BENEFITS AND LIMITATIONS

Cost and time are the two great benefits. Preparing a written report for a client is very time-consuming so few astrologers undertake such work. A well-prepared report of some 20–30 pages would probably take an astrologer at least one and probably two or more days to prepare. At, say £25 per hour, this would be unlikely to cost less than £400–£500, and could cost a lot more. Top astrologers command at least £50 per hour. Furthermore, you may have to wait many weeks for the report. By contrast, it is possible to have one of a range of computer-generated reports, for a cost of about £30, over the counter from, for example, The Astrology Shop, 78 Neal Street, London WC2H 9PA, Tel: 0171–497 1001, or by return of post. Reports range from natal chart analysis, to chart comparisons and reports on your current and future trends.

The limitations of such reports are that they cannot take into consideration your present background situation. Nor do even the best of such reports use more than a fraction of the information in the birth chart, but put together pre-written text for different chart factors. Even with sophisticated computer technology, there are simply too many variables for the computer to begin to simulate the symbolic logic of an experienced astrologer. Thus, even the best reports can omit vital factors in the chart or fail to spot a point of emphasis which would be obvious to even a beginner astrologer.

To date, the one partial exception to this rule are the Astro-Intelligence reports created by Dr Liz Greene, one of the world's most outstanding astrologers and a trained Jungian psychologist, and Dr Alois Treindl, an artificial intelligence expert. These reports are the result of an intensive analysis of the thought processes and interpretative logic of Liz Greene when she is studying a chart. Some of these key processes are built into the program. This ensures that, unlike other such reports at present, the computer assesses the chart as a whole and is able to provide a context in which to place the report. In the future one can expect to see this approach developed further to include an ever wider range of chart subtleties.

INTERPRETATION SOFTWARE

It is also now possible to buy a wide range of computer programs that can produce professional reports for natal charts, chart comparisons and for forecasting. A list of such software can be found in the UT's *Astrology* Yearbook and web site. One of the most economic and elegant of these programs is Adrian Duncan's *World of Wisdom*, available for £50. This is also a valuable self-teaching aid for students. Details on www.world-of-wisdom.com

In addition you will find an enormous range of programs listed in *Astrology*. A few of the most important software suppliers in alphabetical order are given below. Most of these products can be obtained and products demonstrated at Mid-

Heaven Books, 396 Caledonian Road, London N1 1DN. Tel:
0171–607 4133.

Astrolcalc
67 Peascroft Road
Hemel Hempstead
Herts HP3 8ER
Tel: 01442–251809
http://ourworld.compuserve.com/homepage/Astrocalc_UK

Provides a fine, integrated range of modules for all types of
chart calculation and interpretation. These can be added according to your needs.

Astrolabe
32 Glynswood
Camberley
Surrey GU15 1HU
Tel/Fax: 01276 683898

Created by Robert Hand, Astrolabe supplies a wide range of
high-quality software relating to all areas of astrology.

Electric Ephemeris
Omnibus Business Centre
39–41 North Road
London N7 9DP
Tel: 07000 171 666.
Details from http://www.electric-ephemeris.com

A very clear, modestly priced, all-purpose program which
includes the facility to develop one's own interpretation texts.

Janus
from Astrology House
41 New North Road
Eden Terrace
Auckland
New Zealand
Tel/Fax: +64–9–373–5304

One of the latest, best and most comprehensive 'all singing, all dancing' programs available at a relatively modest price.

Matrix
from Library Wing
Abbey St Bathans House
Duns
Berwickshire TD11 3TX
Tel: 01361 840340

Matrix is the pioneer of astrology software created by Michael Erlewine and now offers a comprehensive range of software by many different experts. Details in UK from http://www.astral. demon.co.uk/ and in USA from 315 Marion Ave, Big Rapids, MI 49307 Tel: +616–796–2483 http://thenewage.com

Solar Fire
32 Glynswood
Camberley
Surrey GU15 1HU
Tel/Fax: 01276 683898
email: roy-gillett@dial.pipex.com

This is one of the most elegant pieces of astrology software available for beginners and professionals alike. Created in

Australia by Esoteric Technologies Pty Ltd, PO Box 159, Stepney, SA 5069, Tel/Fax: +61–8–331–3057. This has become something of a world standard which other designers seek to emulate.

WOW
Details on www.world-of-wisdom.com

Adrian Duncan's *World of Wisdom* programs come with a complete built-in atlas enabling one to both calculate charts and interpret them. This is also a valuable self-teaching aid for students as one can 'click and see' around the chart, obtaining on-screen interpretations for each chart feature.

Free Ware
This can be accessed through http://astrology-world.com under 'Freebies'.

If you are familiar with computers and do not mind working with a minimal manual and without on-line support, the best bargain available is the completely free Astrolog 5.3 of Walter D. Pullen, the latest version of which is available for downloading from his web site.

ASTROLOGY ON THE NET

The Net is now populated by an increasing number of invaluable websites dedicated to astrology. If you do not yet have personal access to the Net, do not forget that you can probably obtain access through your local public library. All the sites below include **Links** to other websites. By using these links you will quickly discover the sites that appeal to your

particular interests and approach. Some of the most valuable web sites are:

http://urania.org
This is the website of the Urania Trust which contains the most comprehensive account of astrological information in Britain and around the world *(see above)*. Includes comprehensive lists of schools, courses, organizations, current events, journals, publications and all aspects of contemporary astrology.

http://www.astrologer.com
This is the site run by Dermod Moore of Metalog and offers an invaluable overview of astrology and registered astrologers worldwide. This is the point of access for **The Astrological Association** and the **Centre for Psychological Astrology.**

http://astrology-world.com
One of the best-designed and most informative astrology sites on the Net. Run by Deborah Houlding, this is the home of Ascella Publications and *The Traditional Astrologer* magazine and includes regular updates and links to key sites across the planet including those offering freebies.

http://www.astro.ch
This site, home of the Swiss computer company Astrodienst, provides an absolutely free, state-of-the-art chart calculation service with details of the geographical co-ordinates, time zones and summer time details for tens of thousands of cities, towns and villages around the world. This is also the site for ordering computerized chart reports by Liz Greene, Robert Hand and other fine astrologers.

There is now a wide range of astrological journals around the world in all languages. These are detailed in the Urania Trust's *Astrology* and website *(see above)*. For the English-speaking reader, a few of the most important are, in alphabetical order:

Apollon, The Journal of Psychological Astrology
(Editor: Dermod Moore)
4 Midhope House
Midhope Street
London WC1H 8HJ
email: apollon@astrologer.com

The journal of the Centre for Psychological Astrology contains thought-provoking articles on all areas of contemporary astrology and its interface with depth psychology, ancient and contemporary culture and world affairs. Details on website: www.astrologer.com/apollon Sub details from Mid-heaven Books, 396 Caledonian Road, London N1 1DN.

The Astrological Journal
(Editor: Adrian Duncan)
email: adrian@world-of-wisdom.com
Website: www.astrologer.com/aanet/index.html

Bi-monthly covering all areas of astrology. Subscription free to members of the Astrological Association *(see above)*.

258

Culture and Cosmos, *A Journal of the History of Astrology and Cultural Astronomy*
(Editors: Nicholas Campion and Patrick Curry, Ph.D.)
Website: www.astrologer.com

Twice-yearly. Subscriptions through the Astrological Asssociation and above website. An academic-level journal devoted to the history of astrology and cultural astronomy.

The Traditional Astrologer Magazine
(Editor: Kate Sholly)
P.O. Box 970
Cedar Ridge
CA 95924
USA
Tel and fax: +530–477–8839
email: Subs@MountainAstrologer.com
Website: www.MountainAstrologer.com

An excellent bi-monthly journal which gives in-depth coverage of all areas of astrology. Available in the UK through The Wessex Astrologer, PO Box 2751, Bournemouth BH6 3ZJ.

BIBLIOGRAPHY

GENERAL

Addey, John. *Harmonics in Astrology*, The Urania Trust, 1996

Addey John. *A New Study of Astrology*, The Urania Trust, 1996

Addey, John. *Selected Writings*, American Federation of Astrologers, 1976

Bogart, Gregory C. *Astrology and Spiritual Awakening*, Dawn Mountain Press, 1994

Campion, Nick. *The Practical Astrologer*, Cinnabar Books, 1993

Cornelius, Geoffrey, Hyde, Maggie and Webster, Chris. *Astrology for Beginners*, Icon Books, 1995

Elwell, Dennis. *Cosmic Loom*, The Urania Trust, 1999

Hand, Robert. *Horoscope Symbols*, Para Research, 1981

Harvey, Ronald. *The Spindle of Meaning*, The Urania Trust, 1997

Kruger, Anna. *Astrology: Designs for Living*, Optima, 1989

Parker, Derek and Julia. *Parker's Astrology*, Dorling Kindersley, 1997

Proclus. *The Theology of Plato*, Prometheus Trust, 1996, from 194 The Butts, Frome, Somerset BA11 4AG

River, Lindsay and Gillespie, Sally. *The Knot of Time*, Women's Press, 1987

Rudhyar, Dane. *The Astrology of Personality*, Aurora Press, 1991

Wright, Paul. *Astrology in Action*, Anodyne Books, 1988

THE PLANETS

Costello, Darby. *The Astrological Moon*, CPA Press (vol. 6), 1996

Greene, Liz. *The Astrological Neptune and the Quest for Redemption*, Weiser, 1996

Greene, Liz. *Saturn: A New Look at an Old Devil*, Weiser, 1976

Greene, Liz and Sasportas, Howard. *The Inner Planets*, Weiser, 1993

Harding, Michael and Harvey, Charles. *Working With Astrology*, Consider, 1998

Kirby, Babs and Stubbs, Janey. *Love and Sexuality: An Exploration of Venus and Mars*, Element, 1992

Moore, Thomas. *The Planets Within*, Lindisfarne Press, 1990

Reinhart, Melanie. *Chiron and the Healing Journey*, Penguin Arkana, 1989

Sullivan, Erin. *Venus and Jupiter*, CPA Press (vol. 8), 1988

Tarnas, Richard. *Prometheus the Awakener*, Auriel Press, 1993

THE ASPECTS

Bosman, Leonard. *The Meaning and Philosophy of Numbers*, Rider & Co., 1974

Ebertin, Reinhold. *The Combination of Stellar Influences*, American Federation of Astrologers, 1972

Hamblin, David. *Harmonic Charts*, Urania Trust, 1983

Harding, Michael and Harvey, Charles. *Working with Astrology*, Consider, 1998

Tompkins, Sue. *Aspects in Astrology*, Element, 1989

THE ZODIAC

Goodman, Linda. *Linda Goodman's Sun Signs*, Pan Books, 1973

Greene, Liz. *Mythic Astrology*, Simon & Schuster Inc, 1994

Harvey, Charles and Suzi. *Sun Sign, Moon Sign*, HarperCollins, 1994

Lewi, Grant. *Heaven Knows What*, Llewellyn, 1997

Mayo, Jeff. The Astrologer's Astronomical Handbook, Fowler & Co., 1965

Pagan, Isabelle. *From Pioneer to Poet*, Theosophical Publishing House, 1969

FORECASTING

Hand, Robert. *Planets in Transit*, Pararesearch, 1976

Sasportas, Howard. *The Gods of Change – Pain, Crisis and the transits of Uranus, Neptune and Pluto*, Penguin Arakana, 1989

PSYCHOLOGICAL ASTROLOGY

Greene, Liz and Sasportas, Howard. *Dynamics of the Unconscious*, Penguin Arkana, 1988

Greene, Liz. *The Astrology of Fate*, Allen & Unwin, 1984

Greene, Liz. *Relating*, Thorsons, 1987

Kirby, Babs. *Experiential Astrology*, The Crossing Press CA, 1997

Reid, Linda. *Crossing the Threshold, The Astrology of Dreaming*, Penguin Arkana, 1997

Schermer, Barbara. *Astrology Alive*, The Crossing Press CA, 1988

Sharman-Burke, Juliet and Greene, Liz. *The Astrologer, the Counsellor, and the Priest*, CPA, 1997

THE HOUSES

Herbst, Bill. *The Houses of the Horoscope*, ACS Publications, Inc, 1988

Sasportas, Howard. *The Twelve Houses*, Thorsons, 1985

ASTROLOGY AND HEALTH

Dethlefsen, Thorwald and Dahlke, Rudiger. *The Healing Power of Illness*, Element, 1990

Ebertin, Reinhold. *Astrological Healing: The History and Practice of Astromedicine*, Weiser, 1989

Mann, A.T. *Astrology and the Art of Healing*, Unwin, 1989

GENERAL REFERENCES

Cirlot, J.E. *A Dictionary of Symbols*, Routledge & Kegan Paul, 1985

Peck, M. Scott. *The Road Less Travelled*, Arrow Books 1990

Peter, Laurence J. *Quotations for Our Time*, Macdonald & Co Ltd, 1977

Skafte, Dianne. *When Oracles Speak*, Thorsons, 1997

The Shrine of Wisdom (ed.). *The Divine Pymander of Hermes Trismegistus*, Garden City Press Ltd, 1970